Transformation and Your New EHR

The Communications and Change
Leadership Playbook for Implementing
Electronic Health Records

Transformation and Your New EHR

The Communications and Change Leadership Playbook for Implementing Electronic Health Records

By

Dennis R. Delisle, Andy McLamb, and Samantha Inch

CRC Press
Taylor & Francis Group
Boca Raton London New York

CRC Press is an imprint of the
Taylor & Francis Group, an **informa** business
A PRODUCTIVITY PRESS BOOK

HiMSS®

CRC Press
Taylor & Francis Group
6000 Broken Sound Parkway NW, Suite 300
Boca Raton, FL 33487-2742

Printed on acid-free paper

International Standard Book Number-13: 978-1-138-33126-6 (Hardback)
International Standard Book Number-13: 978-1-429-44740-2 (e-Book)

Visit the Taylor & Francis Web site at
http://www.taylorandfrancis.com

and the CRC Press Web site at
http://www.crcpress.com

Contents

Foreword

There are three truths in American healthcare that are almost so self-evident that they don't need to be stated directly:

1. Healthcare is going to more than incrementally transform over the next several years.
2. Technology will be a huge driver of that disruption as we move from a B2B model to a B2C reality.
3. Electronic health records (EHRs) as they are currently constituted have been disappointing in effecting that change.

While that future is definitely on the horizon, if you are reading this book today you are not living in the future. You are living in a present that can best be described as a "twilight zone" between volume and value, success based on operational efficiency to one based on strategic vision, and, most importantly, a future where data was optional to one where your prosperity and maybe even your survival is the ability to obtain, analyze, and act on a broad set of data and analytics.

Technology in healthcare will be the "secret sauce" and catalyst to transform our world from one in which variability is a given, not only across states or across systems, but in some cases within the same healthcare system or hospital. Data analytics, machine cognition, and augmented intelligence will relegate the anecdotal ways we operate today to an information technology equivalent of the "pre-antibiotic" surgical era.

As crucial as the EHR and other technologies are to effecting that change, even more important is how the humans operating the system react to the process reengineering and how they employ the new insights that are available to them. And that is where this book becomes a must "keep by your side" handbook for anyone contemplating an EHR implementation or improvement (which means just about everyone in healthcare over their career!). And one of the amazing aspects of an EHR implementation is that it magnifies any flaws in a system's culture, morale, or communication. How many times have we heard about a system missing its budget or having some other financial misstep and the CEO "blaming it on the EHR implementation."

A convenient excuse indeed, but a more honest assessment would be, "we missed our budget because I and my team did a poor job of setting a clear direction, engaging the right people in the process and supporting the staff through a difficult and stressful transition." That change leadership model and the communication strategy needed to achieve it is what this book is all about. Jefferson Health is one of the fastest growing academic medical centers in the nation and after five mergers in five years found itself needing to create an interoperable IT solution that would result in One Jefferson. As a safety net hospital with a narrow margin, we knew that our academic medical center implementation needed to reinforce our integration strategy and that any misstep, technical or human, could affect our ability to achieve our goals. In collaboration with our Jefferson leadership team, Dennis Delisle led the change leadership strategy that not only resulted in a successful implementation but now is being copied by other hospitals in the network and other systems throughout the country. That playbook is now available on the following pages in a manner that is customizable, understandable and applicable to any implementation regardless of size.

Having been the CEO of three different organizations that have done massive implementations with three different EHRs, I believe we overestimate the impact of the software and underestimate the importance of the "humanware" necessary to make that software effective. Identifying the stakeholders – both the end users and the staff needed to effect an implementation – is just the first step. Recognizing that each of the stakeholders requires a differentiated communication strategy is often the difference between a successful and a contentious EHR implementation. Just as Super Bowls are won by careful pre-game planning (it's hard not to have at least one Philadelphia Eagles plug), "winning the game" in EHR implementations requires the same kind of planning. How many levels of computer savviness exist with the doctors and nurses in your organization? What are the culture differences between departments? What is the operational readiness of the overall organization? Do the stakeholders believe there is something in it for them or is this just another mandate from administration? The successful resolution to these questions is often based more on how you communicate than the actual answers themselves.

And as Dennis, Samantha, and Andy adroitly point out in the following pages, the go-live date is just the beginning. The need for continuous improvement, soliciting feedback, and sustaining excitement and engagement is way too often overlooked. One of the keys to a successful implementation is "no surprises" before, during, and after the go-live event. This book highlights not only the "why and when" to engage these strategies but the "how" in a very easy to read framework. The "playbook" for implementing EHRs is more than just a title, it is just that. A playbook is meant to be studied and then go back to at different points in the "game." You will find yourself doing just that with this book. Having everyone on the implementation team read it well before the implementation starts, using it as a study guide for the pre go-live, the post go-live, and any troubleshooting or course correction that needs to be considered, and then referring to it for continuous improvement or upgrades will go a long way toward guaranteeing success.

An EHR implementation will always be one of the major gut checks for any organization. Done right, it will serve as a catalyst for transformation in your healthcare system; serve as a unifier for the nurses, physicians, and employees in your hospital or practice group; and, above all, allow you to use data and analytics to drive strategy to better care for your patients. Both mistakes and successes are magnified. It is up to the leaders of your organization to set a clear direction, engage in the process, and support the staff through what is often a stressful transition. This book is a must-have to ensure that the process, the pitfalls, and the people are all evaluated and all scenarios are accounted for. The robust communication plan outlined in the later chapters will ensure that staff, physicians, nurses, and patients are all informed, engaged, and excited about how the technology will improve their workflow.

To paraphrase Jack Ma, CEO of Alibaba, "When cars were created, we didn't try to get humans to run faster. When planes were developed, we didn't teach people to fly. Computers will always be smarter than people…but they will never be as wise. Know the difference between being smart and wise." It is "smart" to implement and continuously upgrade your "computer" through its EHR. But it is "wise" to utilize this book to its maximal potential so that the humans who will make or break the success of the venture have all the tools they need to ensure a successful outcome.

Stephen K. Klasko, MD, MBA
President and CEO
Thomas Jefferson University and Jefferson Health

Stephen K. Klasko, M.D., M.B.A.

Thomas Jefferson University, Philadelphia

Acknowledgments

Our Thanks

We'd like to thank Jefferson Health's President and CEO, Dr. Stephen Klasko, and the leadership teams from Thomas Jefferson University Hospital, Jefferson University Physicians, and the IT department for their vision and transformational leadership during the implementation. Thank you to Praveen Chopra for his insight and wisdom during the most significant change journey in the organization's history.

A special thank you to the EHR Guiding Team co-chairs, SVP and Chief Medical Information Officer Dr. John Kairys and Chief Nursing Officer Mary Ann McGinley, for their guidance and unwavering dedication to the success of this project.

Thank you to the staff of the technical and operational teams who made it all happen, especially the EHR Project Team who built the system from the ground up. Thanks also to Nick Thompson and Kristen Madden for their contributions to the change and communication activities outlined in this book.

Thanks from Dennis

To Dr. John Kairys and Paul O'Connor, thank you for the opportunity to contribute to Jefferson's EHR journey. Your guidance and support were integral to our success. To the EHR Guiding Team, you set the tone for engagement and demonstrated the commitment required to build forward inertia. To my EHR leadership team, Jordan, Joe, Greg, Jen, Renee, Mark, Leslie, and Brian, thank you for your dedication and relentless hard work. The professional accomplishments do not compare with the personal gain of the lasting friendship we developed. To the EHR and IT staff, subject matter experts, and superusers, the organization's success was a direct result of your tireless effort, consistent engagement, and willingness to collaborate. To our operational leaders, especially Rich Webster, Rebecca O'Shea, Sharon Millinghausen, and Shiny George, thank you for your leadership, direction, and support. To Channtoo Chhean, Wanda Holmes, and Rich Faulkner, somehow you were able to manage and coordinate the thousands of meetings, workgroups, and activities that accompany such a comprehensive implementation. To my family, thank you for providing me with love and encouragement throughout the journey.

Lastly, and most importantly, to my wife, Rachel, and my daughter, Ophelia, thank you for supporting my goals and dealing with my long work hours and weekends in the office. You are my inspiration.

Thanks from Andy

Months of effort have gone into preparing the resource you now hold, but the work that shaped it started years ago. There are countless people who deserve my gratitude for being an important part of this book and my life during those years. First of all, my co-authors, Dennis and Sam, two of the most talented and dedicated individuals with whom I have ever had the opportunity to work. Without them, this project would never have been put into motion. Thanks to my family – especially my parents, Tom and Deb, who from an early age helped set my feet upon the rock, taught me to always strive for my best, and encouraged my love of books. I wouldn't have guessed that one day I might see my own name on a cover. Special thanks to my wife, Raquel – more precious than rubies – for her patience through all things. As I draft this acknowledgment, it is late into the evening of our 18th wedding anniversary. She continues to support me every step of the way. Most of all, thanks to God – the author and finisher – who enables me to press ahead, one day at a time.

Thanks from Samantha

To my husband, Geoffrey – I am grateful to be on this journey with you. Our growth mindset philosophy guarantees that we learn from all of life's experiences, and this one was no different. Thank you for being my steady force during the unsteady waves of this implementation. To my parents, David and Theresa – the OG creatives – thank you for exposing me to a diverse array of cultural influences so that I could choose a hybrid path – one that I'm proud to be on today. You've always encouraged my discovery and exploration through writing. In first grade, I would bring you my homemade spy journals and short stories. Now, I bring you my first book. To my friends and colleagues, Dennis and Andy, we've experienced many unknowns, yet one thing remains constant – our open-minded and good-humored working relationship. The combination of our unique strengths has resulted in one of the most memorable collaborations I've ever been a part of.

About Stephen Klasko, MD, MBA

Stephen Klasko is a transformative leader and advocate for a revolution in our systems of healthcare and higher education.

As President and CEO of Philadelphia-based Thomas Jefferson University and Jefferson Health since 2013, he has steered one of the nation's fastest-growing academic health institutions based on his vision of reimagining healthcare and higher education. His 2017 merger of Thomas Jefferson University with Philadelphia University created a pre-eminent professional university that includes top-twenty programs in fashion and design, coupled with the first design thinking curriculum in a medical school, along with the nation's leading research on empathy.

His track record of success at creating and implementing programs that are shaping the future of healthcare earned him a place on *Modern Healthcare's* list of the "100 Most Influential People in Healthcare" and "Most Influential Physician Executives" in 2017. That same year, his entrepreneurial leadership and success at recruiting helped Thomas Jefferson University Hospital achieve a #16 ranking – and elite Honor Roll status – on *U.S. News & World Report's* Best Hospitals list.

Dr. Klasko is a nationally recognized advocate for healthcare transformation, having served as dean of two medical colleges, and leader of three academic health centers before becoming President and CEO at Jefferson. He is the author of 1999's *The Phantom Stethoscope*, 2016's *We Can Fix Healthcare in America*, and editor in chief of the journal "Healthcare Transformation." His new book is 2018's *Bless This Mess: A Picture Story of Healthcare in America*.

Under his leadership, Jefferson Health has grown from three hospitals to fourteen with revenues that have grown from $2.2 billion to more than $5.1

billion, annualized. The new Jefferson focuses on managing the health of populations in southeastern Pennsylvania and southern New Jersey. Jefferson has the largest faculty-based tele-health network in the country, the NCI-designated Sidney Kimmel Cancer Center, and an outpatient footprint that is among the most technologically advanced in the region.

In 2017, this rapid growth led to GE Healthcare signing with Jefferson Health, forming the largest risk-shared partnership in the United States, aimed at saving more than $500 million over eight years.

As of 2018, Jefferson has annualized post-merger revenues of $5.1 billion, more than 30,000 employees, 7,800 students, 6,600 physicians/practitioners, and 4,400 members of faculty.

Through a unique four-pillar model, academic–clinical–innovation–philanthropy, Jefferson has attracted both venture capital and transformational gifts. Sidney and Caroline Kimmel donated $110 million to Jefferson on June 18, 2014, the largest gift in the university's history. Philanthropy and innovation have also resulted in the addition of the Marcus Institute of Integrative Health, nationally recognized for its modern medical and integrated therapies, and the Jane and Leonard Korman Respiratory Institute, a unique partnership between Jefferson Health and National Jewish Health.

Previously, as CEO of USF Health and Dean of the Morsani College of Medicine at the University of South Florida, Dr. Klasko built the nation's largest "assessment of technical and teamwork competence" center known as the Center for Advanced Medical Learning and Simulation (CAMLS). He also led a partnership with the country's largest retirement community, The Villages, to create "America's Healthiest Hometown®," an innovative primary-care-driven, patient-centric, Medicare-based accountable care model.

Dr. Klasko is ideally suited to lead such initiatives, having completed a grant after receiving his MBA from the Wharton School of Business of the University of Pennsylvania on selecting and educating physicians to be leaders of change. His unique medical education program at USF, called SELECT (Scholarly Excellence, Leadership Education, Collaborative Training), is recognized for its focus on choosing medical students based on emotional intelligence and leadership potential.

Dr. Klasko also serves on the board of Teleflex (TFX), an NYSE global medical device company with a market cap of $12 billion. He has served on both the audit committee and governance committee and has been a director since 2008. He is also a trustee of Lehigh University, one of the nation's leading engineering and business schools.

He is married to Colleen Wyse, a fashion leader and founder of the Philadelphia Trunk Show, and has three children: Lynne, David, and Jill.

Authors

Dennis R. Delisle, Sc.D, FACHE Dr. Dennis R. Delisle is a transformational healthcare professional and nationally recognized Lean and change leadership expert. He has a passion for systems thinking, operational excellence, and strategy execution. In addition to national presentations and peer-reviewed publications, Dennis is the author of *Executing Lean Improvements: A Practical Guide with Real-World Healthcare Case Studies.* Dennis is also the Assistant Program Director for the TJU College of Population Health's Operational Excellence Program.

Dennis was the Executive Project Director for the Jefferson Health EHR implementation discussed throughout this book. Along with key IT, clinical, operational, and financial leadership, Dennis was tasked with leading EHR rollout, developing a robust operational engagement model, establishing and facilitating a comprehensive governance structure, and overseeing a continuous improvement program.

Dennis holds certifications as a Lean Master, Six Sigma Black Belt, Change Agent, and Project Management Professional (PMP). Dennis is a Fellow of the American College of Healthcare Executives. He completed his Undergraduate Degree in Biology at Syracuse University, Master of Health Services Administration at George Washington University, and Doctor of Science degree in health systems management at Tulane University.

Currently, Dennis holds a senior operational leadership role at Jefferson Health. He grew up in Branchburg, NJ, and currently resides in Philadelphia, PA, with his wife and daughter.

Andy McLamb, MBA Andy McLamb is the Change and Engagement Management Specialist for Information Services and Technology (IS&T) at Jefferson Health. Andy has strategic responsibility for supporting technology-based change initiatives through centralized IS&T communications – both within the department and between leadership and staff across the Jefferson enterprise. Additionally, he is responsible for creating and executing communications plans for Epic@Jeff, the system's ongoing EHR rollout.

Prior to joining Jefferson Health, Andy held roles as Senior Communications Consultant and Communications Project Manager for health systems implementing Epic. He has a broad range of experience in both healthcare and industry, including past work in corporate communications, digital marketing, traditional advertising, public relations, and event management.

Andy completed his Undergraduate Degree in Business Management with a concentration in marketing at North Carolina State University in Raleigh, NC. He holds an Associate Degree in Computer Science with a focus on networking from Northeast State Technical Community College in Blountville, TN, and a Master of Business Administration degree with a specialization in marketing from King University in Bristol, TN. Andy grew up in Dunn, NC, and currently resides with his wife near Johnson City, TN.

Samantha Inch, CPC, CAPP Samantha Inch is a Certified Professional Coach who helps women in high-stress careers redesign their lives to reduce anxiety, create discipline around well-being, and curate a path to sustainable happiness. Samantha uses her expertise in Applied Positive Psychology to help people create strategies for "high-quality living." Find out more at www.samanthainch.com. Samantha is also bringing a focus on humanity to the workplace. She believes that teaching employees how to manage their minds is the key to an engaged and productive workforce. At Jefferson Health, she has used this approach to create new learning and development curricula, training programs, and wellness initiatives based on the latest developments in neuroscience. Her expertise includes emotional intelligence, stress management, mindfulness, resilience, gratitude, empathy, and growth mindset.

Samantha's background is in the communications field, with an emphasis on storytelling about human connection, motivation, and purpose. With over a decade of experience in Organizational Communications, she has led strategies for Jefferson Health's IT and EHR teams, as well as a multi-billion dollar government defense contractor. Samantha has been the recipient of awards for excellence in communications, including being named on PR News' People-to-Watch list.

Samantha received her Bachelor of Science degree in Communications and Public Relations from the S.I. Newhouse School of Public Communications at Syracuse University. She received her Certification in Professional Coaching from the Institute for Professional Excellence in Coaching, accredited by the International Coaching Federation. She is a proud resident of Philadelphia and lives in Center City with her husband.

Introduction

The *Communications and Change Leadership Playbook for Implementing EHRs* offers a robust communication and change leadership approach to support electronic health record (EHR) implementations and transformation journeys. This book provides comprehensive examples, tools, and templates as a guide for healthcare professionals, with the goal of creating an accessible and useable reference for beginners through advanced practitioners. The communications and change leadership model outlined within was employed at the authors' organization – Jefferson Health – throughout a two-year EHR implementation that included three hospitals, more than 130 ambulatory sites, and 12,000 employees. This book highlights that organization's approach and philosophy of communication, change leadership, and systems and process design, giving readers a practical view into the successes and failures that can be experienced throughout the evolution of an EHR implementation. All content presented was led and managed by the authors.

The Case for Project Communications

The importance of communications should not be underestimated, as they are essential to the successful adoption and implementation of your electronic health record. While routine communications activities are part of every team member's responsibilities, you must be prepared to supplement those individual, day-to-day activities with a carefully crafted and consistently implemented communications strategy for the enterprise and project as a whole.

Some enterprises might propose reducing or eliminating dedicated communications resources, or dispersing the responsibility for communications activities among other roles such as project managers, directors, or application analysts. While that approach can result in short-term savings, it can also compromise the overall success of your EHR project by introducing constant distractions for key leaders and team members who need to focus on critical project-related tasks. Such a shortsighted approach rarely results in the consistent or effective execution of communications plans, often creates missed opportunities, and in some cases can result in costly delays. Many organizations that make the decision to minimize communications resources at the outset to reduce costs will recognize mid-project that an important gap exists. At that critical point, precious time and resources are often required to secure communications support.

These pitfalls can be avoided by prioritizing and staffing communications needs appropriately as part of the earliest discovery and planning phases of your EHR project. During those initial planning phases, a strong focus on communications will add unique value and much-needed creative energy to your project. The benefits you will start to see will take on a life of their own throughout the project and well beyond.

In This Book You Will Find

A high-level overview of key communications strategies and principles including specific details about:

- Overarching communications and planning strategies
- Key audiences who should be engaged
- Primary messaging points for specific audiences
- Timelines for critical project activities and related communications
- Practical real-world examples
- Hints, tips, and lessons learned from previous implementations

To help guide you through the playbook, the following icons denote helpful hints, tips, and other callouts that warrant additional consideration. Keep your eye out for them!

 Lessons Learned and Quick Tips

 Case Studies and Examples

Useful icons.

Who This Book Is For

The playbook is primarily intended for individuals who are responsible for transforming health systems through EHR implementations, including professionals within information technology (IT), clinical and financial operations, project management, and senior leaders. It was also developed to appeal to other health professionals who will be able to utilize its straightforward and practical approach to tools and content, including technology analysts, clinical informaticists, frontline managers and supervisors, process and quality improvement teams, undergraduate and graduate professors teaching EHR strategy and IT courses, and students in all related health professions.

Audiences should keep in mind that while this playbook offers a model for planning and executing communications and change leadership strategies – including key project phases and common deliverables – it does not cover all details of your EHR implementation execution. Instead, it is intended to be an accompanying and supplementary resource to a robust project plan. Additionally, some tools and content may not be appropriate or relevant to all readers. It is important to take your organization's culture and history into context when reviewing the material within this guide and to adapt the approach to fit your needs.

How This Book Is Organized

When reviewing this playbook in its entirety, you will notice some repetition of themes and elements from one section or chapter to the next. That is because the playbook has been designed to be picked up and referenced at any given point, without needing to read multiple chapters – or the entire guide – for context. If you are seeking information or examples for a specific stage of your EHR implementation, you will find those materials embedded directly in the chapters alongside accompanying explanations.

Starting in Chapter 1, the Communications and Change Leadership model is introduced. That framework outlines key communication goals along the continuum of transformational change and suggests tools and content to engage and inform stakeholders. As a basis for the guide, the model will be outlined and detailed throughout the remaining chapters, providing the reader with a coherent understanding of the ongoing strategy and approach. Three phases of change (Current, Transition, and Future) serve as the foundation of the communication strategy, and six core phases (Vision, Plan, Engage, Train, Prepare, Launch) comprise the major categories of project activity. The following integrated model is designed to facilitate your planning across each stage of the change and project execution continuum in a thoughtful, structured manner.

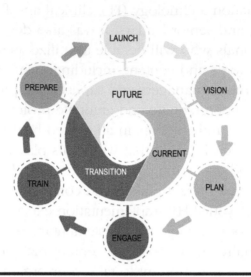

Communications and change leadership model.

Chapters 2 and 3 emphasize the Current Phase period within a change initiative. Along with defining the vision, your main focal point during that time will be stakeholder engagement. Chapters 4 through 5 review the Transition Phase, a critical state of interim change. Because the Transition Phase represents a move away from the status quo toward the defined vision, you should expect it to be one of the tensest times for all involved. End-user training, recruitment of support resources, and operational readiness activities will be essential to reducing stress and tension for your stakeholders.

The Future State represents go-live and beyond. During the Future State, the inertia you have generated through earlier stages of the project will help support change as staff adjust to a new way of doing work. Preparations and stakeholder engagement that have been put in motion throughout the project will converge at this point, and technical and operational readiness will be a top priority as your go-live approaches. Chapters 6 and 7 focus on important go-live communications for your EHR, as well as what happens afterward. Once live on a new system, there must be a shift toward issue resolution, system enhancement, and long-term optimization. The partnerships you develop with clinical and operational leadership and subject matter experts will continue to be leveraged as teams work together to prioritize resources and improvement efforts to align with broader organizational goals. Keep in mind that, throughout all stages of your EHR implementation, communication and change leadership strategies should be consistently evaluated and improved to ensure messages are appropriately conveyed and received.

By the time you finish this book, you should have the knowledge and tools required to design and execute a robust Communication and Change Leadership strategy. We hope you find the information herein informative and actionable, and we wish you the best of luck as you embark on your transformation journey!

Chapter 1

Overview of Communications and Change Leadership Model

Change, whether incremental or fundamental, is difficult. When it comes to the implementation of a new electronic health record (EHR), the status quo for your organization may be completely upended. Therefore, your strategy and approach for change leadership must take culture, individual and collective perception, and historical context into consideration. Effective communication is at the core of that change leadership. A thoughtful, well-executed communication plan accompanied by efficiently managed project implementation will lead to the engagement, support, and adoption of your new EHR. Conversely, failing to execute in these critical areas can be catastrophic.

You should be aware that transformations of this magnitude require significant investment in a robust communication and change leadership strategy to ensure individual and organizational success. The change process can be defined in three distinct phases (Figure 1.1):

1. Current Phase
2. Transition Phase
3. Future Phase

The Current Phase represents how things are today, the status quo. The Future Phase is the time when your defined vision is brought to reality. Between those two lies the Transition Phase. Understanding how individuals work through a new change requires an understanding of each phase. By

Figure 1.1   Phases of change.

identifying any areas of opportunity or risk, you will position your EHR implementation for success.

 Change has a considerable psychological impact on the human mind. To the fearful, it is threatening because it means that things may get worse. To the hopeful, it is encouraging because things may get better. To the confident, it is inspiring because the challenge exists to make things better.

Anonymous

Current State

The Current Phase is comfortable and predictable, representing how things are today or "the way we've always done things." In order to generate the momentum needed to shift away from this comfortable state, you must establish a sense of urgency and create a clear vision for the future (Figure 1.2). Here are key questions that you should consider when crafting your change leadership strategy:

Making a Case for Change
- Why do we need to change?
- Why does it have to happen now?
- What could be improved over how we do things today?

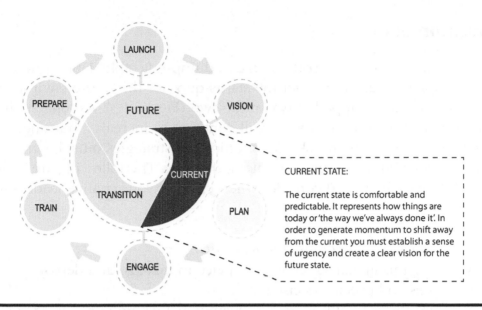

CURRENT STATE:

The current state is comfortable and predictable. It represents how things are today or 'the way we've always done it'. In order to generate momentum to shift away from the current you must establish a sense of urgency and create a clear vision for the future state.

Figure 1.2   Current state.

- What is better about the vision and future state than what we have now?
- Are there specific threats or opportunities that create additional urgency for change?
- What are the primary barriers to challenging the status quo?

Defining a Vision
- What should the future of the organization look like from the perspective of patients, providers, staff, and other stakeholders?
- How will we define success?
- What are our guiding principles during this time of change?
- Who is leading the effort, and how will senior leadership be engaged?
- What teams and partnerships do we need to develop or leverage?
- What changes will the new vision prompt for specific individuals, teams, and departments?

Communications Considerations
- Who are the target audiences we need to reach (individuals and groups) and what are their information and communication needs?
- What key messages need to be relayed to the appropriate stakeholders?
- What modes of communication will we use (e.g., email, website, fliers, presentations)?
- When and how often will communications and messages be delivered?
- How will we solicit feedback and drive bidirectional communication?

Transition State

The Transition Phase is uncomfortable and unpredictable. During this phase, employees are in neither the status quo nor the future environment, but may feel trapped between the two (Figure 1.3). As long as the future remains uncertain, anxiety will continue to increase. Transitional periods are times of high risk. Communication strategies must be created to support and reassure staff along the way. The following are some key questions you should consider when crafting your change leadership strategy:

Stakeholder Assessment and Management
- What organizational structure is in place to manage and deploy resources and execute decisions?
- Who are the natural leaders (i.e., champions) within our organization?
- What governance bodies will provide oversight and decision making?
- What team building and relationship development activities are needed?
- How will the EHR team develop effective partnerships with clinical and financial operations?
- What areas or issues require intervention from senior leadership to ensure forward progress?

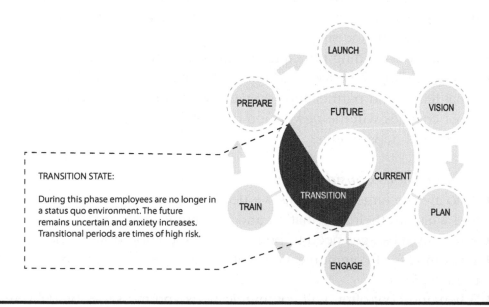

Figure 1.3   Transition state.

Stakeholder Analysis

- Who are the key stakeholders, and what is their level of support or resistance?
- What influence strategies need to be developed to ensure support and engagement?
- Are physicians (employed and non-employed) engaged and onboard with proposed changes?
- How will we regularly solicit feedback about the perception of our EHR implementation (e.g., surveys, open forums)?
- What bidirectional feedback tools will we use to ensure effective communication and participation?

Operational Readiness

- How will we determine the operational impacts of our EHR implementation?
- What are the potential implications for existing policies or procedures?
- What key organizational risks need to be evaluated (e.g., workflows, data migration, training needs)?
- Are there any current organizational processes, structures, or other factors that could be potential barriers to our success?
- What operational teams need to be established to drive acceptance and readiness both broadly and at local levels of the enterprise?
- How will we document current state workflows and determine gaps between current and future states?
- How will we evaluate operational and organizational readiness throughout the implementation?

Training and Engagement

- What is our training strategy (e.g., who, when, how)?
- Will unique training be required to meet the needs of different end users?
- Do we have sufficient training space to accommodate the entire end-user community?
- What training aids or other materials will be needed to supplement in-class or web-based courses?
- Do we have workflows or other processes that could be changed before the go-live to make that process easier?
- Is there a roadmap of role-specific activities that can be executed in preparation for the go-live (e.g., playground scenarios, simulations, dry runs)?

- Are there any established engagement or feedback forums we can use to solicit staff perceptions of change and readiness throughout the implementation?

Performance Feedback
- How will we celebrate success throughout our transition?
- What interim goals or project milestones can be shared to highlight forward progress?
- How can we recognize individual and team contributions?
- How will we create transparency and demonstrate progress on a regular basis?

Communications Considerations
- What feedback do we want to receive from end users – either formally or informally – regarding their perception of the changes?
- Are there specific individuals or end-user groups (e.g., nurses, physicians, lab techs) who are struggling or more resistant to change than others?
- How engaged are senior leaders and operational stakeholders, and who among them should be advocates and voices for the changes we are making?
- Do any themes exist around common gaps or issues across departments or end-user groups?
- Are the communication modes (e.g., email, website, presentations) we use generally effective and well-received throughout the enterprise?

Future State

The Future Phase represents an ideal. For some, it can appear as a wishful dream, while for others it is a realistic aspiration (Figure 1.4). The future state should serve as the "North Star" for your EHR implementation. That constant direction will help align individuals and teams toward a common goal. From a change leadership perspective, the future vision will create excitement and instill hope. From the EHR perspective, the upside of new technology means improved patient experience, physician engagement, and user satisfaction – as well as increased productivity. The following are key questions you should consider when crafting your change leadership strategy:

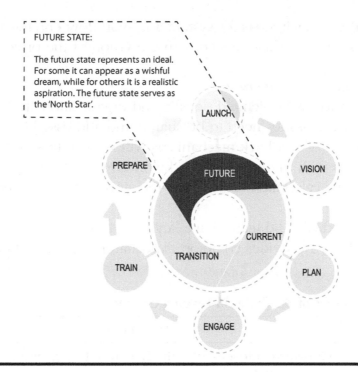

Figure 1.4   Future state.

Launch (Go-Live)
- What should be our target go-live date?
- What are the key milestones and strategic timeline?
- How will we assess go-live readiness (e.g., technical and operational)?
- What support systems and processes will we put in place during go-live and on an ongoing basis (e.g., help desk, command center)?
- What operational transition plans need to be developed and implemented?
- What is our post-live stabilization and sustainability plan?
- What is our strategy to train, retrain, and provide technical assistance to rapidly address any issues we encounter?
- How will we determine compliance and adoption metrics?
- What key performance indicators will we use to measure success?

Continuous Improvement
- How will we define ongoing system improvement and change control processes?
- How will we document and integrate lessons learned as we go?
- Are there tools, features, or functionalities we deferred that will be implemented after go-live?

- How will we solicit ideas for system and workflow enhancements?
- Is our post go-live state aligned with the vision of the project?

Communications Considerations
- How will success be defined (locally and organizationally)?
- What risks and issues need to be shared and addressed broadly?
- What forums or feedback mechanisms will we use to solicit end-user experiences with the new tools and workflows?
- How will we celebrate big wins and recognize key contributors?

Various individuals and teams have key roles throughout the EHR implementation. Table 1.1 provides common expectations of these stakeholders:

Table 1.1 Examples of Key Roles in Leading Change

Role	Expectations
Senior Leadership	• Provide context for how the EHR fits into organizational transformation • Generate organizational buy-in • Establish EHR governance structure
EHR Governance Member	• Communicate vision and strategy • Identify and appoint individuals to participate based on their role, expertise, credibility, leadership • Establish long-term objectives and targets and allocate resources • Ensure organizational systems, structures, and process drive culture
Operational Leaders	• Assess readiness for change • Remove implementation barriers • Facilitate communication across disciplines
EHR Leadership	• Remove implementation barriers • Develop and foster team building within EHR teams and operations • Provide structure and processes to identify, escalate, and resolve issues • Provide transparent updates on progress • Allocate resources to address EHR implementation needs and risks
EHR Project Team	• Support end users • Partner with operations to ensure alignment and readiness • Identify and escalate issues and concerns

Communications Framework

The Change Leadership Model serves as a foundation to over-lay the Communications Framework. Figure 1.5 depicts the six major communication phases for EHR implementations. Communication tools and approaches, which will be described in subsequent chapters, are based on each phase:

1. *Vision* for the project (Chapter 2)
2. *Plan* for the change (Chapter 3)
3. *Engage* end users and operations staff (Chapter 4)
4. *Train* users for the changes (Chapter 5)
5. *Prepare* operational and technical areas for go-live (Chapter 5)
6. *Launch* the new system (Chapter 6)

Once live on your new EHR, the vision that you established initially should continue to evolve to meet new needs and leverage technology in different ways. This iterative improvement cycle is essentially a refresh of the Change Leadership and Communication Model, emphasizing life after go-live with a focus on system and workflow enhancement (Chapter 7).

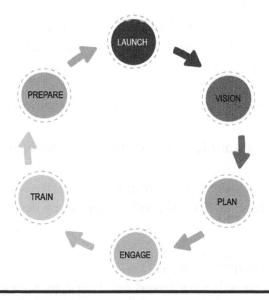

Figure 1.5   Communication phases.

Communications Infrastructure

The importance of communication during an EHR implementation warrants a dedicated team. Because communications will vary by mode, audience, and frequency based on a complex set of constantly changing needs, an experienced, agile group will be needed to manage and execute. The following are recommended roles for the Communications Team. If your organization is not able to staff a dedicated team, it is important to designate specific individuals with these responsibilities:

Communications Lead
- Dedicated solely to the EHR implementation and is a member of the EHR leadership team
- Embedded within the Project Team and responsible for determining, consolidating, and disseminating key messages
- Participates in leadership meetings to align communication messages with priorities established by EHR governance and leadership
- Provides advisory support and consultation to EHR leadership and project staff for decentralized (i.e., day-to-day) communications activities

Communications Staff
At least one full-time equivalent (FTE) or experienced consultant is highly recommended to support the communications lead with the following responsibilities:

- Contributes to the development and dissemination of communication materials
- Maintains key communication channels (e.g., websites, newsletters, updates)
- Is embedded within key workgroups or teams to solicit ideas, key messages, and feedback on the effectiveness of communications activities

Communications Team Structure
Size and structure will vary based on the project scope. Align the team with the EHR leadership's structure, as shown in Figure 1.6:

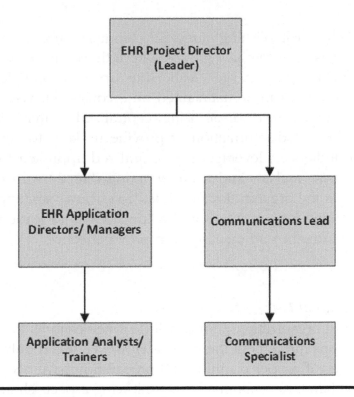

Figure 1.6   Communications team structure.

Communications Infrastructure

When starting a communications plan, it is important to evaluate and understand your enterprise's existing communications infrastructure, including:

■ Hierarchy and processes
■ Channels and methodologies
■ Distribution lists
■ Key audiences
■ Primary influencers and approvers

The Communications Team will need to work with leadership to help reinforce existing communications channels and effectively communicate with key audiences throughout the project. The following aspects must be carefully considered during the planning process.

Centralized versus Decentralized Communications

Establish parameters and set expectations for how centralized, decentralized, and targeted messaging will be used throughout the project.

When establishing targeted communications, identify and focus on a few key groups where those efforts will have the greatest impact (i.e., leadership updates, provider updates, etc.) and can be maintained on a consistent basis with high-quality messaging. Instead of using centralized communications to share highly detailed information or provide updates to very small or specialized audiences, leverage a decentralized approach through the EHR application analysts and teams working directly with operations. Depending on the organization, a robust "roadshow" strategy with EHR leadership taking key messages and talking points to leadership meetings and department staff meetings can prove effective.

Email Distribution Lists

Within most organizations, email will be a key channel for communications throughout the project. However, it can only be used effectively if proper planning and preparation have been completed beforehand. At a minimum, the following aspects should be addressed:

■ What email distribution lists already exist, and what lists need to be created or updated – leadership, providers, nursing staff, different "waves" of staff for go-lives, or other groups?
■ During what project phase will each distribution list need to be used, allowing adequate time for preparation?
■ Who will own each distribution list, for the purpose of maintenance and regular updates?
■ How often should each list be updated based on turnover or anticipated staffing changes?
■ If there are multiple email systems across your enterprise, how do distribution lists need to be built and what parameters should be used to accommodate each system?

Role of Leadership and Operations

It is important for senior leadership and operations to understand and affirm their ownership of key decisions and communications throughout the project. This includes:

- Owning system decisions, workflow changes, and project activities
- Cascading important messages and reinforcing communications to staff members locally at all levels of the organization
- Providing feedback about what is working well and where opportunities exist for more effective engagement and communications activities
- Engagement in leadership-driven project meetings, such as operational readiness

While a leadership structure likely exists to support communications activities informally, that structure may need to be formalized, enhanced, or reinforced to ensure appropriate messaging occurs at all levels throughout the enterprise. Consider the following aspects:

- Who are the key subject matter experts and operational leaders?
- Which leaders typically support communications activities, engage staff, and provide consistent and useful feedback when requested?
- Where do additional communications champions need to be developed throughout your enterprise to address any communications gaps?

Communications Review and Approval Process

Depending on the type of communication and the channels being used, different leaders will need to be part of the review and approval process. In order to streamline the vetting process and avoid unnecessary delays in your communications, that structure should be established in advance. Be sure to consider the following individuals (if applicable) for review and approval:

Executive Communications – System Level
    Examples: Executive memos to all staff, video messages from C-Level, etc.

- Chief Executive Officer
- Chief Medical Officer
- Chief Nursing Officer
- Chief Operations Officer
- Chief Financial Officer

- Chief Marketing Officer
- Chief Communications Officer
- Chief Medical Information Officer
- Chief Nursing Information Officer
- Chief Information Officer
- Other C-Level Executives (or Executive Vice President [EVP], Vice President [VP], as needed)

All Staff and Operational Communications – System Level
Examples: Project newsletters and updates, operational leadership talking points, etc.

- EHR Project Director
- EHR Application Directors or Managers
- EHR Application Analysts or Trainers

Leadership Communications – Project Level
Examples: Leadership memos to Project Team, regular team updates, etc.

- EHR Project Director
- EHR Application Directors or Managers
- Chief Medical Information Officer
- Physician Champions

Team Communications – Project Level
Examples: Project Team reminders, working messages, updates from the project management office, etc.

- EHR Project Director
- EHR Application Directors or Managers
- Project Management Office

Provider Communications
Examples: Updates for physicians, mid-level providers, etc.

- Chief Medical Information Officer
- Chief Medical Officer
- Physician Champions
- EHR Project Director

Patient Communications
   Examples: Patient portal marketing, patient experience communications during go-lives, etc.

■ EHR Project Director
■ Chief Marketing Officer or Marketing Directors

Communications Timing and Project Milestones

Table 1.2 shows a cross-section of a communications timeline. To create a working plan and align frequency and timing for various communications and project activities, this type of chart should be expanded when key dates and deadlines are available for content collection, creation, review, approval, and dissemination.

Communications Channels

The following list outlines a wide range of communication channels that you can use throughout the EHR implementation:

Electronic Channels
■ Email
   – Newsletters and updates
   – EHR and senior leadership memos
■ Intranet Website (Figure 1.7)
   – Dedicated website for EHR implementation
   – Featured images and rotating carousel highlights
   – Regular news feeds
   – Inpatient- and ambulatory- specific updates
   – Training and resources
■ Electronic "Signage" – Visible by staff and patients.
   – Televisions
   – Computer screensavers
■ Online Surveys
■ Print Channels
   – Poster boards
   – Newsletters
   – Fact sheets
   – Fliers and posters

Table 1.2 Example Communication Timeline

Category	Month 1	Month 2	Month 3	Month 4
Roadshow Presentation	• Senior leadership presentation • Monthly operational workgroup presentations	• EHR governance presentation • Monthly operational workgroup presentations	• Senior leadership presentation • Monthly operational workgroup presentations	• EHR governance presentation • Monthly operational workgroup presentations
Website	• Important project milestone updates	• Highlight EHR feature/ functionality	• Important project milestone updates	• Highlight EHR feature/ functionality
Newsletter/ Email	• Timeline update • Look ahead: new features/ functionality of HER	• Timeline update • Key upcoming tasks and engagement activities	• Timeline update • Look ahead: new features/ functionality of HER	• Timeline update • Key upcoming tasks and engagement activities

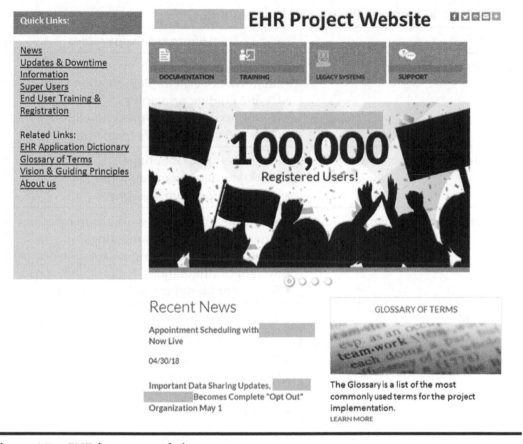

Figure 1.7   EHR intranet website.

Personal Channels
■ Slide decks and talking points for:
  – Roadshows
  – Leadership meetings
  – Operational meetings and huddles
  – Grand rounds and provider meetings

EHR Implementation Phases

Some EHR vendors provide a structured plan for "standard" installation, which is typically divided into several general phases. Each phase includes unique activities that will require varying levels of communication and engagement with audiences throughout your organization. Key activities are

Table 1.3 Key Project Phases and Deliverables

Phase	Key Milestones/Deliverables
Project Scoping	• Establish governance • Identify/staff EHR implementation team • Define guiding principles • Define scoping and project timeline • Operational site visits/gap analysis
Strategic Direction	• Key stakeholder meetings • Workflow alignment sessions • Workflow redesign sessions
System Configuration	• Subject matter expert workgroup meetings • Operational readiness meetings • Preparations for training • System Configuration • Superuser identification/preparation
Testing	• Technical application/integration testing • End-user acceptance testing
Training	• Operational readiness • Superuser training • End-user training • Workflow demos/ simulations
Launch (System Go-Live)	• Activation of new system
Support/ System Enhancement	• Scheduled maintenance downtimes • System enhancements/upgrades/updates • Improvement projects

listed in Table 1.3, and a more detailed communications breakout by phase can be found in subsequent chapters.

This outline uses generic terminology that should be applicable across EHR vendors. Because the phases of your EHR project may span months or even years, and your primary and secondary audiences will likely change during each phase, communications strategies should be evaluated and adjusted regularly to ensure they remain effective. Table 1.4 provides a sample Gantt overview of an EHR implementation timeline. A similar project timeline should be used to inform your communication strategy and priorities based on incremental progress, issues encountered, and anticipated

Table 1.4 High-level Project Timeline

Key Activities	Year 1				Year 2			
	Jan–Mar	Apr–June	July–Sept	Oct–Dec	Jan–Mar	Apr–June	July–Sept	Oct–Dec
Project Kick-off	■							
Site Visits/Workflow Assessments		■						
Workflow Validations		■						
System Configuration			■					
Testing				■	■			
Training				■	■	■		
Operational Readiness Activities							■	
Launch/Go-Live							■	
Continuous Improvement								■

Table 1.5 Centralized Communications Timeline

June	July	August
• Testing • Superuser activities • Operational readiness • Featured executive: CMO • Featured providers: OB Nurse	• Testing • Training and registration • Workflow demos • Operational readiness • Featured providers: Radiologist	• Training and registration • Patient safety • Superuser activities • Operational readiness • Featured providers: Medical oncologist
September	**October**	**November**
• Training • Cutover • Superuser activities • Introduction to go-live readiness • Featured providers: Emergency medicine physician	• Training • Go-live readiness • Command center overview • Featured executive: CEO	• Go-live readiness • Command center details • Training • Superuser details • Post go-live updates

challenges. This type of overview roadmap will help all parties, technical and operational, understand where the project is, where it is heading, and what to expect along the way.

Table 1.5 is an example of a more detailed centralized communications timeline. This type of document is helpful for Communications Team planning and provides a look-ahead for key topics based on the timing of key activities and events. It should include any items that require at least 1–2 months lead time to execute, as well as specific content to ensure operational readiness.

Based on your implementation and communications timelines, additional information should be provided to stakeholders, when appropriate. Table 1.6 and Example Communication 1.1 provide an example of project milestone details, including high-level description, purpose, timing, and operational commitment. Remember to provide your operational counterparts enough lead time to accommodate staff participation in strategic activities – especially for clinical areas, physicians, and providers.

Table 1.6 Example of Project Milestone Details

Milestone	Description	Purpose	Timeline	Subject Matter Expert (SME) and/or Operational Commitment:
Hardware Testing	Technical teams will test all existing and new devices to ensure they work as expected with the new EHR.	To document the workstation placement, area layout, access needs, equipment deficits, infrastructure concerns, etc.	October–April	• One (1) manager level person to touch base with prior to, and possibly during, the testing. • Estimated 1 to 4 hours of time in the department and time for the SME's involvement (time will vary based on the size and operational complexity of the department). • Note: The department will be contacted in advance to identify the Project Team's key contact during the visit and schedule an appropriate, least intrusive time for the walkthrough of the area.
System Configuration	Customization and refinement of the new EHR to reflect operational needs.	To translate all validated workflows, orders, lists, documentation, tests, schedules, etc., from earlier gap analyses and alignment sessions.	October–July	• Hundreds of SMEs will be involved in the configuration process. Contributions range from a minimal touch base for clarification purposes only to gathering and sharing department data to review and validating the final configuration. • Required hours vary by session.

(Continued)

Table 1.6 (Continued)   Example of Project Milestone Details

Milestone	Description	Purpose	Timeline	Subject Matter Expert (SME) and/or Operational Commitment:
Superuser Program	Superusers will serve as an extension to the EHR Project Team. The superuser role will be comprised of operational and clinical staff who have additional training and responsibilities in preparation for go-live.	Provide "at-the-elbow" support (i.e., at the bedside, clinic, workstation) during and post Go-Live. They are the first line of defense for troubleshooting and managing any workflow issues in real time for frontline staff.	Recruitment begins January. Superuser training: Sept–October Go-live Support: November–December	• Go-live support: At-the-elbow with end users for 2 to 4 weeks after go-live. • Total number of hours will be determined based on the superuser's area of coverage (final schedule based on number of end users, superusers available, and hours of operation). • Total number of days and hours of commitment will be dependent on the success of end-user adoption and proficiency in the superuser's area.
Data Conversion	Electronic transfer of specific items from previous legacy systems into the new EHR, completed by Project Team, and validated by operations.	To capture unique data elements from legacy system files that will be needed for future patient care.	October–November	• Approximately 3–5 hours are required depending on each SMEs area(s) of expertise, authority for approval, and quantity/type of data each will be assigned to review.

(Continued)

Table 1.6 (Continued)   Example of Project Milestone Details

Milestone	Description	Purpose	Timeline	Subject Matter Expert (SME) and/or Operational Commitment:
Training	All end users will be required to attend training before they will be granted access to the new EHR.	Ensure staff are adequately trained to use the system in order to return to normal operating levels as soon as possible.	October–November	• Specific number of training hours will vary by end-user role. • Classroom training times: Provider 8–12 hours, support staff 4–20 hours.
End-User Testing	Coordinated testing of the build by operational resources.	To ensure, from end-user perspectives, that the design reflects intent, validation points, and intended usage.	September	• 4 to 16 hours for test data entry and result validation.
Go-Live Readiness Assessments	Meetings with operations and Project Team that are scheduled 30, 60, 90, and 120 days prior to go-live.	Strategically scheduled to assess readiness before go-live.	Monthly: August–November	• 4 to 16 hours of preparation for session report outs. • Three, 1-day sessions will review readiness for go-live, requiring 4 to 8 hours for operational representatives.

(Continued)

Table 1.6 (Continued)   Example of Project Milestone Details

Milestone	Description	Purpose	Timeline	Subject Matter Expert (SME) and/or Operational Commitment:
Cutover Activities	Preloading of specific information into the new EHR system by technical and operational resources.	Information is needed for clinical patient care, to maintain previously scheduled appointments, to maintain established workflows such as provider schedules, treatment plans, etc.	November	• 4 to 16 hours dependent on quantity of data, number of interfaced systems/operations owned, third-party systems, and vendor staff.
Go-Live	Official date that we turn on the new system.	Established date allows for proper timing and sequencing of events that are needed for successful implementation and function.	Wave 1 Go-Live: November 1	• EVERYONE!!

Example Communication 1.1: Project Timeline Overview

Title: Project Timeline Overview
Mode of Communication: Email
Target Audience: All Staff
Sent From: Project Team

The Project will progress through a series of carefully planned phases:

- *Planning and Scoping (complete)*
- *Kickoff and Current State Assessments (complete)*
- *Validation and Reengineering*
- *System Build*
- *Testing, Training, and Go-Live*
- *Continuous Improvement*

Planning and Scoping (Complete)

A cross-functional team of leaders and experts came together for months of planning. This Project Team identified more than 90 workflows that have posed challenges in other EHR implementations, and those workflows were documented for reference.

The organization established project governance and decision-making processes along with a comprehensive methodology to monitor project plans. Additionally, more than 800 SMEs from across the enterprise were identified to help support the project.

During this time, the scope of the project was defined. This included the identification of specific EHR applications that would be implemented and what systems would be replaced, establishment of an overall project budget, and formation of the working Project Teams.

Kickoff and Current State Assessments (Complete)

The project kicked off with a series of engagement events attended by employees, leaders, and members of the community. During this time, the Project Team also conducted hundreds of Discovery Site Visits in order to learn more about the current state of workflows and processes.

Validation and Reengineering

Starting in July and continuing through October, Validation Sessions will be conducted. These sessions provide the opportunity for SMEs to review and finalize the EHR workflows needed to build our new system. The fourth round of Validation – also known as Reengineering – will follow Validation to review and approve any workflows that require revisions after the initial review. During this time, Training Team members will attend various sessions and begin gathering information in preparation to update their lesson plans for future training activities.

The decisions made during this phase will be operationalized by the Project Team as it builds clinical content for the workflows.

System Build

The Project Team will build the new system during this phase. The team will also complete the necessary preparations for system testing to ensure everything works as planned. Most of this work is done behind the scenes by the Project Team. Updates will be provided on a regular basis so everyone will know when key System Build milestones are accomplished.

Testing, Training, and Go-Live

During this phase, the new system will be tested thoroughly to ensure it works as designed. As the Project Team prepares for the Go-Lives in both ambulatory and inpatient environments, special scripts will be used to test the system's workflows for accuracy. These scripts will be repeated as needed until each application runs smoothly.

During this time, principal trainers will train end users – nearly all staff – to use the new EHR. The Project Team will also perform Go-Live Readiness Assessments at 90-, 60-, 30-, and 15-day checkpoints prior to Go-Live.

Then, We Will Go-Live!

All systems being replaced will be turned off in coordination with Go-Live events.

Continuous Improvement

The implementation process does not end with the Go-Live. After that time, support and system improvement, including issue resolution and ongoing user education, will be our primary focus. This phase also includes a number of visits by Project Team staff to assess our implementation and satisfaction with the product and process.

Additionally, functionalities and workflows that were deferred until after Go-Live will be optimized during this phase. Enhancements will also be made to further improve the new system.

To meet future needs, our journey during this final phase will continue far beyond Go-Live through continued stabilization, optimization, upgrades, and the adoption of future applications. Our journey is just the beginning of the future for us as we continue to deliver exceptional care to all those we serve.

Chapter 2

Vision: Current State Baseline Assessment and Strategy Development

The visioning phase and associated assessment and strategy development include many activities (Figure 2.1). Your implementation will usually kick off following a vendor decision from senior leadership and the Board of Directors. After this point, you will kick off the initial change and communications activities with employees. During this earliest phase, leadership teams and governance structures will be formed, as well as the hiring and onboarding of Project Team members. Throughout this phase, you should ensure that key leaders are updated about the status and timeline of key decisions.

At the same time, a change and communications assessment should be conducted in preparation for the creation of the project communications plan. A high-level vision for the project must be established and communicated to all employees, and you will likely want to invite key stakeholders and leaders to an official project kickoff event. The overall messaging during this time period should begin to focus on positive, long-term benefits that will change your organization's future for the better (Table 2.1).

Introducing the People

Key Objectives and Message Points

Communications about the governance structure for your implementation will be important to set expectations and assure those involved that there

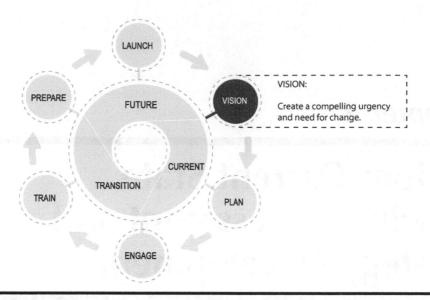

Figure 2.1 Vision.

are checks and balances for major decisions, as well as to keep track of the overall health of the project.

Communications about the hiring and onboarding of Project Team members is important as leadership establishes the project's organizational structure and internal communications processes; sharing those types of details will help satisfy the concerns and interests of high-level leaders and stakeholders who are eager to understand how the project ecosystem is being developed.

Additionally, focusing early communications efforts on the team will inject a human interest component that can help add life and credibility to the communications and other activities that will follow.

The following message points will be important to use with end users and providers. Remember that messaging should always be framed within a context that fits the culture and communications strategy of your unique organization.

- There will be a strictly organized governance structure that will inform key decisions about the way we implement our EHR software and how the system impacts associated changes to our operational workflows. Questions or concerns about decision-making processes can be directed to the governance teams.
- Members of the Project Team will build and deliver our new EHR system to the organization. You will have opportunities to meet our team

Table 2.1 In This Section

Activity/Event	Primary Objectives	Key Messaging Points	Communications Tools
2.1 People	Introduce the structure and people of the governance teams and the Project Team.	• There will be a strictly organized governance structure that will inform key decisions about the way we implement the software and associated changes to our operational workflows. • The Project Team is your frontline who will build and deliver the system to the organization.	• Email updates to leadership teams invested in the hiring process. • Intranet articles accessible to all employees that paint a human interest story so the project leadership is relatable. • Meetings: Establishment of governance meeting cadence as well as Project Teambuilding activities to encourage early communication.
2.2 Assessment and Strategy Development	Use a hybrid approach of: 1) External research, in the form of benchmarking other organizations about their success and failures; and 2) Internal surveys to assess your organization's needs based on cultural nuances.	• We are conducting organizational benchmarking and best practices to position ourselves for the best possible implementation. • We are taking your feedback and communications preferences into consideration to inform our strategy.	• Emails: Update employees on the objective of surveys, invite them to take the surveys, and inform them of the results.

(Continued)

Table 2.1 (Continued)   In This Section

Activity/Event	Primary Objectives	Key Messaging Points	Communications Tools
2.3 Defining the Vision	• Focus on explaining and communicating the project at a high level – setting basic, simple, and clear expectations and answering the 5Ws. • Early communications should focus on creating a positive dialogue and positioning the new system as the catalyst to progressive change rather than a negative disruptor.	• Here is our overarching vision for our organization 5, 10, and 20 years from now. • The benefits of the system will be first and foremost our patients. Next, our clinicians will benefit through an increased focus on safety, operational efficiencies, and streamlined access and communications. • Here is a summary of the communications plan and what you can expect to see about the project.	• Emails and intranet stories: Early communications, preferably from the executive level, should focus on establishing the need for change and how the change can be successful. • Decentralized meetings: Operational leadership should reinforce informally through huddles and meetings directly with staff. • Event: Project kickoff to educate, engage, and celebrate.

members and leaders through interviews, as well as working with the various application teams and understanding how they will operate.

Communications Tools

- Email updates
  - Share updates about the governance structure and the hiring progress: It is important to recognize internal momentum as the team comes together.
- Intranet and newsletter
  - Human interest features about project members and the leadership team will help paint a picture of where they come from and why they are excited about charting this new path for the organization.
- Meetings
  - In addition to your governance meeting structure, onboarding and teambuilding activities will strengthen relationships and begin the process of EHR education (Example Communication 2.1).

Example Communication 2.1: EHR Governance Structure Created for Efficient Decision Making

Title: EHR Governance Structure Created for Efficient Decision Making
Mode of Communication: Email
Target Audience: All Staff
Sent from: Project Team

With any major organizational change, it is important to establish a structure that enables project decisions to be made in a timely and effective manner – this is known as governance. As the team continues to plan for the implementation of {NAME} organization's new Electronic Health Record, they have defined a governance process where decisions will be made about issues such as workflow planning, system design principles, and specific departmental applications. Patients and families will be at the center of every decision. At this time, the governance structure includes the following:

Guiding Team: This team was assembled and introduced in {TIME PERIOD}. Since then, this group of enterprise leaders has helped oversee and guide the pre-implementation planning activities.

Work Groups: The Guiding Team has broken out into a set of {QUANTITY} work groups to tackle pre-implementation projects such as defining the overall project strategy and approach, establishing the governance structure, managing change readiness activities, and preparing for technology, reporting, and analytics needs. These teams have made great progress laying the foundation for the official kickoff of the project this summer.

Advisory Teams: {QUANTITY} advisory teams will provide operational expertise and use standard methods and tools to make timely and critical decisions.

Subject Matter Experts (SMEs): SMEs will be working closely with the Advisory and Project Teams to offer guidance and expertise during the decision-making process. A few months ago, the community was encouraged to apply for official SME positions and represent their department during implementation. The Project Team is currently finalizing those lists and confirmations will be sent to the selected SMEs in the coming weeks. The team is also developing detailed guidelines to share with SMEs about their involvement going forward.

People who do not become official SMEs at this time still have the opportunity to offer feedback and input during the lifecycle of the project. Nearly all departments will have a designated SME to serve as a liaison between their department and the Project Team.

Project Management Office: The PMO is a support function for the Project Team and will help manage a variety of tasks through a standardized set of processes, methodologies, and tools. The Project Team will rely on the PMO to keep them on time, on budget, and on scope.

As always, all feedback is welcome. Please send an email to **{NAME}** and it will be addressed by a member of the Project Team.

Assessment and Strategy Development

As the first governance meetings begin and your Project Team hiring and onboarding progresses, you can begin your change assessment to get out in front of potential areas of concern and understand what communication gaps need to be filled. You will want to assess existing forums to use as interim communications vehicles while you are developing your overall communications strategy. Finally, you should create and explain your overarching communications plan to employees to set expectations on how they can expect to receive information about the implementation. There are usually two components to this assessment. The first is an external benchmarking of other organizations through research, or "client calls" and interviews. Your EHR vendor should be able to help you get in touch with other organizations to discuss best practices. The second is an internal assessment that takes your organization's specific culture into account. There are numerous free online tools that can be used to conduct surveys and set up informal focus groups to gather metrics about what people want and expect to get from your change and communications initiatives.

Objectives and Key Message Points

- ▪ We are conducting organizational benchmarking and best practices to position ourselves for the best possible implementation.
- ▪ We are taking your feedback and communications preferences into consideration to inform our strategy.

Communications Tools

- ▪ Surveys: Various survey tools are available online with free or paid options. Many times, a free account will be sufficient. Surveys should be kept brief (10 questions or less) with a combination of multiple choice and comment boxes to achieve the best possible survey response (See Example Communication 2.2).
- ▪ Emails: Update staff on the objective of your surveys, provide deadlines and reminders, and be sure to inform them of the results.
- ▪ A simple chart that outlines the key activities while you are building out full communications plans. This can be used to review your priorities in the interim period between setting up governance and launching your communications strategy (Table 2.2).

Table 2.2   Example Communication Outline

Hiring (Through March)	Focus on face-to-face communications based on HR's success with personal and targeted conversations Feature human interest stories about recent hires
General Timeline Updates (Through May)	Execute organized and quality communications to translate goals, promote progress, and address employee concerns
Development of Full Communications Plan (Through May)	Create a targeted audience strategy with drumbeat promotion of milestones, team progress, and successes

Example Communication 2.2: Potential
Internal Employee Survey Questions

 Title: Change and Communications Assessment Survey for
employees
Mode of Communication: Online Survey Tool
Target Audience: All Staff
Sent from: Project Team
Change and Communications Assessment Survey for employees

Communications Questions:

- How informed do you feel about the EHR project and how you fit into the process?
- How frequently would you like to get information about the EHR project?
- Do you have any other feedback?

Change Management Questions, Please Rate
the Organization's Ability To:

- Communicate the need for change.
- Define what will change and how it will impact the organization.
- Organize staff and workflows to help drive successful implementation.
- Identify the right people, processes, and data to assess progress and sustainability.
- Do you have any other questions or concerns?

Defining the Vision

In the earliest phases of your implementation, most staff will have little or no working knowledge of the new EHR. What they do know may be influenced largely by their feelings about current or past systems or details obtained from (potentially negative) media stories or other staff who have used an EHR elsewhere. Therefore, getting out in front of those perceptions with strategic messaging is very important. Remember that there will be naysayers and skeptics, as with any change initiative.

Key Objectives and Message Points

Develop a communications plan that spans the duration of your project timeline. Following your project's official kickoff, you will need to be prepared to launch various components of the plan (e.g., intranet site, roadshows to leadership and staff meetings, newsletters) to maintain momentum. Some key components include the following:

- Centralized (owned by the communications team at the enterprise level) and decentralized (owned by project leadership teams to align with their local operational counterparts) plans for disseminating information throughout the enterprise.
- Project name, theme, and branding (i.e., "look and feel"), with approved logos (normal and reverse) and various file formats (raster and vector). To avoid confusion and nomenclature changes mid-project, establish a naming convention and style for individual areas that will complete go-lives at different times (i.e., if you are not doing a "Big Bang" implementation). For example, terms such as "Wave 1" and "Wave 2" should be used to denote sequential launches that involve different areas of the enterprise.
- Timeline and major project milestones requiring awareness or action from employees.
- Messaging and themes per phase and for specific project milestones (build, training, go-live, etc.).
- Champions and spokespeople established at various levels and departments who have direct influence with key segments of the organization.
- Push and pull communications tools and related communications channels where employees indicated they would like to get information and other updates.
- A feedback mechanism for staff to get in touch with general questions or comments for the Project Team. The communications team should field initial questions and help draft final answers with support from appropriate subject matter experts.

Internal content pipelines and approval processes should be established between the communications team, technical experts, and project leaders to help translate important messages and provide approvals in real time. Consider a few key activities as you establish your processes:

- Embed: Communicators are neither clinical nor IT/systems professionals. Understanding content will require immersion with the project management office (PMO) and application managers. Develop working relationships to address these gaps.
- Partner: Identify subject matter experts who will begin to understand and support the "future state" vision. Those champions should help

translate what types of behavior and workflow changes will be required for the new EHR system – and share how those benefits will impact key user groups.

- Define: Identify what will be different in the future state for each core user type (e.g., physicians and providers, nurses, scheduling and front desk staff, back office staff, etc.) and any potential areas of confusion. You should understand the details of key project milestones so those can be mapped back to your communications timeline.

 At this early stage where the credibility and voice of the C-suite is needed to establish the vision, high-level leadership (VP, CMIO) co-working processes and approvals are necessary. However, you may want to find an intermediary between the communications team and the C-suite level to approve non-executive level memos, intranet articles, and other real-time, urgent communications that cannot wait for a high-level approver. We found the executive project director or a delegate was the best solution.

Depending on your organization's past experiences with technology roll-outs or other implementations, you may need to establish why this experience will be different (i.e., better) than others have been.

The following message points will be important to use with end users and providers. Remember that messaging should always be framed within a context that fits the culture and communications strategy of your unique organization.

- How much planning has gone into making the decision to proceed?
- Who has been involved in the evaluation process, and who will be leading and involved with the EHR implementation moving forward (i.e., Executive Guiding Team, Project Team, operational leaders, subject matter experts, etc.)?
- What type of budget has been allocated for the EHR implementation?
- What benefits are anticipated from implementing the new system?

Overarching Vision Messages

- To succeed and to survive in the future, our organization must become a data-driven, continuously learning enterprise.

- This project is a foundational element to our organization's success in the coming years.
- This is not just a technology project, but a transformational journey for our entire enterprise.
- Don't be afraid to think differently and do things differently. We must be faster, smarter, and deliver greater value to our patients and their families.
- Our new EHR system will help us drive the delivery of world-class, patient-centric, and clinically integrated inpatient and outpatient care.
- Overarching benefits of our new EHR system will include improved efficiency, stronger financial tools, seamless scheduling and patient education capabilities, and helpful demographics and analytics that will provide critical insights into how we manage and treat the populations we serve. Bottom line, it will improve experiences for us and for our patients.
- Each year, we collect data from more than **{QUANTITY}** patient visits, **{QUANTITY}** admissions, and **{QUANTITY}** surgeries. By using our new EHR system, we will be able to streamline that data to help make better decisions for the future of our business.
- Over the next few years, this initiative will touch all areas of our enterprise.
- The investment we are making during the implementation of this new EHR is monumental. We are doing this for the benefit of you and our patients.

Communications Tools/Activities

- Intranet: You should position an internal project website as a one-stop-shop – the destination source for all news and updates, including archived news and updates. The website should be one of the first tools you set up as a home base for the early adopters who want to learn more. Of course, you should ensure that your site aligns with your implementation project name and branding.
  - Some types of information you can begin including on your project website include interviews and introductions with leaders, overviews of your EHR vendor and key terms, a high-level timeline and milestones, project leadership and governance structure, etc. There may also be resources from your vendor that can be repurposed for use on the project website.

- Emails: Until you implement a formal electronic update tool such as an electronic or printed newsletter, be sure to provide email updates. Remember, email updates should always prioritize quality over quantity.
- Events: Host a formal "project kickoff" event for key operational, clinical, and financial leadership to learn about the vision from the project leadership team. Key spokespeople should include your CEO, CIO, CMIO, hospital presidents, and other operational leaders.
  - A sample event agenda is as follows:
    - Welcome
    - Why are we doing this? What is our current state?
    - Introduction of governance and key stakeholders
    - Guiding principles and overarching rules for the project
    - High-level timeline and key project milestones
    - Opportunities and challenges
    - Lessons learned from other organizations
    - Next steps, how you can stay informed and involved

See Example Communications 2.3–2.5 on the project kickoff event and the post-kickoff recap.

 Project Kickoff Event – You may also want to invite an external organization from your benchmarking studies to be a guest presenter i.e. another CIO or CMIO from a like-minded organization that has completed a successful install. This gives the attendees assurance that an undertaking of this magnitude has been accomplished successfully elsewhere.

Example Communication 2.3: Project Kickoff, Discovery, and Validation

 Title: Project Kickoff, Discovery, and Validation
Mode of Communication: Email
Target Audience: All Staff
Sent from: Project Team

Save the Dates

We'd like to thank those of you who participated in the change readiness survey, which closed last week. We received more than **{QUANTITY}** submissions and we're looking forward to reviewing your feedback and sharing a summary soon. Our overall momentum around the new EHR is growing and we can see your excitement reflected in the overwhelming response to job postings over the past several weeks. The Project Team is nearly 80 percent complete!

Our readiness activities are in full swing as we prepare the organization to take an active role in implementation. There are three critical milestones we'd like to bring to your attention today. These milestones include the **Project Kickoff, Discovery Site Visits, and Validation.**

Over the next several weeks, we will begin to identify and engage SMEs – leaders and end users from across the institution who will help design the future state of the system. We will request many of you to act as SMEs and your attendance will be required at the following two events:

The first is the **Project Kickoff** and subsequent **Discovery Site Visits.** Those of you who become SMEs will be invited to the kickoff meeting to learn more about the timeline and expectations going forward. Following the Project Kickoff, SMEs will lead department walkthroughs and participate in roundtable discussions with the Project Team. Discussions will focus on current workflows and opportunities to improve workflow design. Invitations will be sent out at a later date.

The second milestone is known as **Validation.** During this event, the Project Team will demonstrate the integrated software to the SMEs who will critique and validate the future standardized workflows. During a series of four Validation sessions, the Project Team and the end-user community will better understand their roles in preparing the organization to use these new workflows.

Example Communication 2.4: Invitation to Project Kickoff

Title: Project Kickoff Invitation
Mode of Communication: Email
Target Audience: Managers and above
Sent from: CIO and/or CMIO

Project Kickoff Event: Please join **{NAME}** organization's EHR project leadership to commemorate the official Project Kickoff on **{TIME<PLACE}**. During the event, senior leadership will be joined by **{VENDOR}** representatives to provide an overview of the project, discuss our progress to date, and outline expectations and next steps.

During the second hour, **{VENDOR}** representatives will lead a demonstration of the latest system. This part of the program is optional.

Example Communication 2.5: Project Kickoff Recap

Title: Project Kickoff Recap
Mode of Communication: Intranet Article

Target Audience: All Staff
Sent from: n/a

> This is the start of a consumer-driven revolution that we will
> be a part of – not reacting to but leading. And you are all the
> revolutionaries. – CEO

The kickoff was attended by more than **{QUANTITY}** senior leaders, deans,
department chairs, project governance members, the Project Team, and
many other members of the community.

The morning began with a new video and a welcome by **{CIO}** who
highlighted the significance of the day in the organization's history. He
then introduced **{President and CEO}**, who took the stage to reinforce the
importance of the system to our future as a leader in healthcare.

"The main thing I want to convey is that this is not a **{VENDOR}** implementation," he/she said. "Like everything else we do, this is going to be part
of a transformation."

Watch the introductions and remarks below.

Next, a presentation by **{CMIO and Chair of the EHR Guiding Team}**,
{CNO}, and {Co-Chair} emphasized that this project will affect all of us,
and asked for engagement from all staff.

For the full presentation, watch the video below.

What followed was a lively presentation by guest presenter **{NAME}** from
{NAME} organization.

"Doing one of these projects gets into every part of what you do – your
professional, personal, and family lives," he began as he told an anecdote
about his young daughter.

His presentation showed that it is not only possible for **{VENDOR}** to
be successfully implemented, but that it can be done on time, on budget,
and on scope. His encouraging words stressed that with proper planning
and a comprehensive approach, the implementation will be effective and
streamlined.

{INSERT LINK TO VIDEO REPLAY.}

The second hour of the kickoff was spent in a live demonstration of a
patient's care continuum within the system.

Chapter 3

Plan: Developing Stakeholder Buy-In

Immediately following your electronic health record (EHR) kickoff event, you should have generated some buzz for your implementation. Following that event, you will have a prime opportunity to launch formal communications across the enterprise. In the months that follow, your organization will complete several project milestones, and the Project Team will begin to build the new EHR system. During that time, a key role of communications will be to continue fostering organizational buy-in for the project. You should focus on educating stakeholders about core capabilities of the new EHR system, preparing staff and subject matter experts (SMEs) to take ownership of departmental planning, and encouraging operational engagement in strategic activities and the finalization of new workflows (Table 3.1 and Figure 3.1).

Communications Strategy and Launch

Key Objectives and Message Points

Because many of your stakeholders will have different preferences for how they want to receive communications, you will likely find benefit in creating a multimodal communications plan. At the start of your project, you will want to make a "splash" with the launch. Later in the project, you will need to tie everything together to demonstrate:

Table 3.1 In This Section

Activity/Event	Primary Objectives	Key Messaging Points	Communications Tools
3.1 Centralized vs. Decentralized Communications Plan and Strategy Launch	• Create and represent a cohesive centralized plan and tell employees what they can expect and rely on including a regular cadence of emails, intranet updates and meetings vs. the information they will receive through their local channels.	• You can expect to hear the latest updates and requests for your participation through our monthly communications cadence. Influenced by your feedback, we are launching the "Pulse" newsletter, our one-stop-shop intranet, and a monthly meeting roadshow as our primary channels. • You can expect your application team leaders to update you more regularly with specific requests for your involvement or updates for your department.	• Newsletters • Project intranet website • Hard copy flyers and other fact sheets for areas not accessible by computer • "Roadshow" presentations at key meetings • Brand campaign and visual recognition (i.e., logos, graphics, color palette)
3.2 Targeted Physician Engagement	• Physicians are one of the most important yet most challenging audiences to engage, and without their buy-in, the project can suffer. Segment your physician population early to meet their communications needs separately.	• What are the top need-to-know items that impact physicians directly? • What are their concerns and how can you address them head-on? • What meetings or validation sessions do you need their participation in?	• Monthly physician-specific newsletters or talking points documents • "What to expect" physician buy-in overview info packets

(Continued)

Table 3.1 (Continued)   In This Section

Activity/Event	Primary Objectives	Key Messaging Points	Communications Tools
3.3 Early Adopter Engagement and Involvement in System Workflows	• System demos: Show end users what the system looks like in advance of training so they can better prepare themselves between kickoff and training. • Prior to building the system, there must be a diverse representation of subject matter expert participation in the validation of new workflows.	• It is important for us as an organization to spend time evaluating workflows and how they will impact current processes throughout the enterprise. • Spending sufficient time and engagement now will help reduce rework and confusion during system build and later phases.	• Email invites to demos • In-person demos • Executive memo about validation sessions • Email invites to validation sessions • Meetings/presentations for validation sessions • Session survey/follow-up mechanism

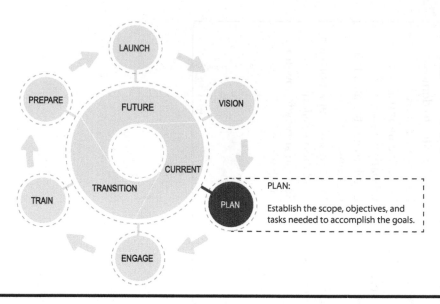

Figure 3.1　Plan.

- The development of a thoughtful and long-term approach to informing, educating, and instructing the organization toward success
- The consideration of feedback from staff surveys
- The comprehensive coverage for all channels of communications (in-person, email, web, video, hard copy) based on different preferences and job roles

Over time, your messaging will evolve past the high-level vision and overarching system benefits to the next level of detail about awareness and education regarding your new EHR system and specific workflows and processes. That evolution should include a review of key system terminology and overviews of various applications within the system. Keep in mind, despite the fact that we are working with technology, it is always important to maintain a human element in your communications (because talking only about the EHR system will make it more difficult for people to see the benefits, and will not generate as much engagement).

Be sure to balance your system messaging with key updates about the team's hard work, interviews with subject matter experts who are excited about the positive changes the system will have on their job and their patients, and recaps of successful decisions and events to demonstrate quick wins. The following message points will be important to use with end users and providers. Remember that messaging should always be framed within a context that fits the culture and communications strategy of your unique organization. You can expect to hear the latest updates and requests for your participation through our monthly communications. Influenced by your feedback, we are launching a newsletter, a one-stop-shop intranet site, and a monthly meeting roadshow as your primary sources of information.

■ Post-kickoff, we invite and encourage you to learn more about the system. Make it a part of your staff meetings and discussions with your peers to encourage assimilation and limit overwhelm. We have provided numerous resources to get comfortable with the system and the impending changes to your workflows. You can always contact our general communications mailbox with questions, and we will ensure you get a timely answer.

You can expect your project application team leaders to update you more regularly with specific requests for your involvement or updates for your department.

Communications Tools

Centralized:

■ Electronic newsletter: Distributed via an all-staff email every month.
■ Intranet site: Catch-all for news, updates, archived newsletters, videos.
■ Hard-copy flyers and posters for TV screens: Due to the nature of clinician roles, you want to take advantage of quick-read, user-friendly vehicles including flyers for nursing unit community boards, TV screens located around the hospital, etc.
■ Meetings: Begin a project roadshow and increase ambassador presence at key stakeholder meetings (Table 3.2).
■ Brand campaign: After the initial launch of your project name, logo, and brand visuals, you will have several opportunities to launch a mid-project campaign to maintain momentum. During lulls in visible project activity, it will be important to keep everyone aware that the project is still actively moving forward.

Table 3.2 Example Roadshow Schedule

Meeting	Attendees	Frequency of Meeting	Project Team Presenter	Confirmed to Present?	Jul	Aug	Sept	Oct	Nov
Management Update	Operational and clinical managers/directors	Monthly	Project director	Yes	X	X	X	X	X
Clinical Enterprise Meeting	Chairs, administrators/VPs, medical directors	Monthly	CMIO	Yes	X	X	X	X	X
Ambulatory Administrators Meeting	Administrators	Monthly: Third Wednesday at 1:30–3:30 pm	Project director	Yes	X	X	X	X	X
Rehab Dept. Staff Meeting	Physical therapy (PT), occupational therapy (OT), speech, rehab aides, support staff	Monthly: Fourth Wednesday at 1:00 pm	Application manager	Yes					
Pharmacy Leadership	Pharmacy management team	Every Tuesday from 10 am to 12 noon	Application manager	Yes	X	X	X	X	X
Nursing Key Personnel	Nurse managers, nurse education, clinical nurse specialists (CNSs), nursing vice presidents (VPs), professional development	Monthly	Application manager	Yes	X	X	X	X	X
Access/Revenue Advisory Committee	Committee members	At least monthly	Revenue cycle application manager	Yes	X				

Decentralized:

■ Application teams should establish their own meeting structure with their respective departments.
■ Subject matter experts and validation sessions (while the Communications Team will support executive messaging, invites, and follow-ups) may be more effectively managed in a decentralized fashion through the Project Team and with facilitation from your EHR vendor.

Physician Engagement

Key Objectives and Message Points

You may realize early on that, based on the niche needs of your physician population, a different level of communication and engagement strategy will be required. That will likely include a mix of centralized and decentralized communications with support from the Communications Team, project leadership, and physician leadership.

You will also want to ensure you build an early rapport with key physician leaders, and collect the names and emails of department chairs and other clinical leaders to ensure you can quickly execute targeted electronic communications to physicians and providers when necessary.

The following message points will be important to use with physicians and providers. Remember that messaging should always be framed within a context that fits the culture and communications strategy of your unique organization.

■ What are the top need-to-know items that impact physicians directly?
■ What are their concerns and how can you address them head-on?
■ What meetings or validations do you need their participation in?

 Depending on your culture, you may find a newsletter format is not suited to your providers. In previous experience, we found that after a provider newsletter, which lasted for 2 months, feedback was given that providers and physicians would rather hear directly from their leadership. Therefore, a more robust meeting/talking points strategy can cut to the chase much more effectively. While you might continue to offer the information in multiple ways, it may serve you better to ask directly what this group wants and create a mutual accountability agreement in using what is provided.

Communications Tools

- Monthly provider newsletter (See Example Communication 3.1).
- Physician engagement meetings: A physician engagement team may be formed, consisting of department chairs and other influencers meeting on a regular basis to make progress toward involving and educating staff across all departments.
  - To kick off this type of campaign, your physician engagement team can divide and conquer to host one-on-one meetings with department chairs – laying out expectations, providing key updates, and filling requests for additional information about upcoming project activities.
  - You can also create a one-time engagement document to use as a handout during these meetings. This type of physician engagement guide will help pull together disparate information into a single packet to review documentation, key dates, talking points, and other workflow-related updates. This summary approach is a good way for department chairs and high-level leadership to get on board.
- Monthly emails: Monthly emails containing talking points that outline the top 3–5 most important things to know for that month, including a specific call to action. This document can be compiled by the Communications Team with support from project leaders, and reviewed by the physician engagement team for edits and additions before sending to your department chairs to customize for their departments. Table 3.3 provides an example of this type of document. The point of creating this type of template is to make communications and engagement as simple as possible for the busiest leaders and staff. To execute effectively, you should ensure an efficient review process and set expectations with your stakeholders to meet the editorial deadlines.

■ Roadshow: You will want to adjust your ongoing monthly roadshow strategy for the physician community. Optimally, project physicians should be available to present, to lend credibility to your message, and help answer questions appropriately.

■ Videos: Based on the time constraints of physicians, video interviews can be a simple and user-friendly way of communicating with physicians. Using a relatively inexpensive video camera, begin to capture quick snippets of system testimonials from physicians that have either used the system before at another health organization, or can speak to its benefits in a way that provides credibility and weight where written communications cannot.

Table 3.3   Example Talking Points for Physician Leadership to Use with Their Staff

Topic	Talking Points	Call to Action
Physician Compensation Model/RVU Impact	Physician participation in required EHR activities will not penalize RVU attribution. RVUs will be allocated and counted toward RVU-based productivity compensation and will be assigned when clinical time is canceled to allow attendance at required meetings.	It will be the responsibility of the clinical department's leadership to approve the RVU allocations.
Hardware and Workstation Spaces	The Project Team, IT, facilities, and clinical staff are evaluating and planning for upgrades and new hardware needs to accommodate workflows and capacity. The objective is to standardize as much as possible.	Please work with the project staff when they visit your department and feel free to raise questions.
Additional Resources	A physician engagement guide will be distributed to each department chair in the Jan/Feb timeframe.	Physicians, please reach out to chairs for more information.
Departmental Notes/Comments:		
(Insert additional talking points specific to your department/area here)		

Example Communication 3.1: Provider Newsletter

Title: Provider Involvement Key to Avoiding Confusion
Mode of Communication: Provider Newsletter
Target Audience: All Providers
Sent from: CMIO
Provider Involvement Key to Avoiding Confusion
A Special Update From the CMIO

Summary: This is a call to action for you, our colleagues. We are asking for your involvement and input to help determine how the EHR is built – for us and our patients.

During our time working with the EHR as part of the Guiding Team and as Operational Owners in these initial stages of validation and development, we have drawn some early conclusions. The EHR will be a vast improvement over what we use now on a daily basis, but it isn't a perfect solution for providers.

In order to make the EHR the tool we need, we must all become more involved in the planning process. That is especially important now, as the system is designed and we begin preparing for change through the clinical operational readiness team.

Here are two key observations from our experiences to date:

- There is nothing quite as big as what we are starting. That is why it is valuable for us to come together to give feedback and link up with others to solve significant problems through the EHR.
- As we scanned the rooms during recent valdiation activities, we observed that providers, despite being invited, remain underrepresented.

You might have read or heard about a recent article from October 22, in the New England Journal of Medicine entitled "Transitional Chaos or Enduring Harm? The EHR and the Disruption of Medicine." The article, which is linked to this update, highlights potentially negative impacts that can result from implementing EHR systems, including confusion and inefficiency for providers.

We appreciate the significant work that many physicians and other providers have already been putting into the planning process. But as we begin to make specific decisions about how our new system will work, we need even more providers to participate and share ways that the EHR can support them in patient care every day.

Early Adopter Engagement and Involvement in System Workflow Decisions

Key Objectives and Message Points

Consider partnering with your EHR vendor to host system demos to provide a closer look at the new system and its functionality. The vendor personnel may actually put on a show and become "actors," portraying nurses, physicians, and other clinical roles while they walk through the experience of using the system with a mock patient. These demos may be the first time your audience can actually visualize the system components and envision themselves engaging with it in the future. While you cannot expect all employees to attend or participate, those who do may actually start to serve as ambassadors for your messages.

At this point in your project, messaging does not call for active participation from *all* end users (that ask will come during the second half of the project when employees are required to train and prepare specific operational plans). You will start smaller, with a call for employees to become SMEs to help make workflow decisions in advance of system build or superusers to support go-live.

These activities are where the real interest starts. You will notice engagement start to gain traction as subject matter experts help review and approve workflows, and then talk about their experiences with their colleagues. Because workflow adoption is a piecemeal process and one of the first stages of the implementation, subject matter experts might find it difficult to form opinions about the overall system or a specific application. Centralized communications and consistent leadership talking points should be used to help fill the gaps, get ahead of negative rumors, and provide positive messaging.

 Set your expectations early. Despite efforts to explain the purpose of workflow review, adoption, and other preparatory activities, many individuals may still have trouble understanding the long-term impacts of individual workflow decisions they are being asked to make until later in the project. Time commitments requested from operations at this early stage can begin to result in resistance and frustration from leadership and staff. Keep this in mind when creating communications.

The following message points will be important to use with end users and providers. Remember that messaging should always be framed within a context that fits the culture and communications strategy of your unique organization. It is important for us as an organization to spend time evaluating workflows and how they will impact and change current processes throughout the enterprise. The investment of your time and engagement now will help reduce rework and confusion during system build and later phases of our EHR implementation.

Other Key Message Points to Address:

■ What is the purpose of workflow adoption activities?
■ Why are so many meetings required during this time?
■ When do activities occur and who will be required to participate?
■ What are some of the additional benefits of the system, including high-level introductions to applications, features, and functionalities?

Communications Tools

■ Email invites to demos
■ In-person demos
■ Executive memo about validation sessions
■ Email invites to validation sessions
■ Meetings and presentations for validation sessions
■ Session surveys and follow-up mechanisms (See Example Communication 3.2–3.6)

Example Communication 3.2: Intranet Article Recapping Vendor Demo

Title: EHR Vendor Demo
Mode of Communication: Intranet Article
Target Audience: All Staff
Sent from: Project Team
VENDOR Demonstrates Software to Community during Interactive Overview Sessions

Last week, the newly selected EHR provider visited campus to lead demonstrations of the new software. The CMIO and Chair of the EHR Guiding Team, **{NAME}**, opened each session with an introduction.

"The world of healthcare is changing right in front of us – it is this fact that makes this project one of the most important things we will be doing on this campus over the next 10 years," he said. "We all understand how critical it is to support the continuum of care for our patients because they are at the heart of everything we do. This makes this process not only a technical transformation, but a transformational journey and key part of our growth strategy."

The vendor facilitators began to tell the audience a real-time "story" of three different users interacting with the system – a patient, physician, and nurse.

As the patient formatted his personal mobile device to the big screen in front of the auditorium, session attendees, who had up to this point been attentively listening, began to get louder with excitement. The screen showed his movements as he accessed his records, reviewed recent test results, set up preferences for email or text notifications, checked refills on his medications, messaged his care team, and scheduled appointments with his physician.

Next, the physician and nursing scenarios began. The physician accessed his mobile device from a remote location where he was efficiently able to address the patient's real-time needs. He viewed charts and lab results, signed scripts, and closed the process by documenting notes via voice recognition. At the office, the physician accessed his dashboard for data management where he could view patient flow, schedule and room updates, and physician quality metrics.

This story continued for the next hour, where detailed demonstrations showed the advanced capabilities, ease of use, and convenience of the new software. Most importantly, attendees saw firsthand the significance of how one consistent EHR makes it easy to follow a patient. This is a monumental improvement by **{NAME OF ORGANIZATION}**, who is planning full implementation for primary and specialty, inpatient, and outpatient care.

For more information, visit the new "one-stop-shop" for all EHR news, located at the **{WEBSITE}**. You can also find out more about EHR job opportunities on the HR website.

Example Communication 3.3: Memo About Discovery/ Validation and How You Can Be Involved

Title: Workflow Discovery and Validation
Mode of Communication: Email
Target Audience: All Staff
Sent from: Project Team

To establish a strong foundation for the project, a set of guiding principles was created. One of the principles states that all stakeholders should "Participate, Engage and Respect." Those involved in Discovery Site Visits and Validation will be asked to participate and engage while maintaining respect for all members of the team. These two milestones are critical to prepare the organization for the system build beginning later this fall.

Discovery Site Visits

- **What/When:** {VENDOR} staff will be on site for educational and informational discussions known as Discovery.
- **Why:** During these preliminary site visits, {VENDOR} staff will learn our workflows so they can identify the areas where {VENDOR} can solve problems, generate more efficiency, and improve satisfaction for both employees and patients. This information will help the Project Team create the foundation for Validation and product build-out.
- **Who:** Operational leadership and our newly designated SMEs will participate in discussions and offer candid feedback about what workflows currently work well and which ones could use improvements.
- **Where:** Roundtable discussions will be set up at varying locations across campus.

Validation Sessions

- **What:** After the Discovery Site Visits are completed and {VENDOR} staff understand the intricacies of our operations, the implementation team will collect all feedback and pre-implementation documentation, risk analyses, fitness tests, and other data to prepare for Validation where {VENDOR} will propose new, existing, or improved workflows. Validation sessions are organized by application and the workflows discussed will be those that significantly impact application build and frontline staff. By the end of the four Validation sessions, we will have finalized more than {QUANTITY} key workflows.
- **Why:** Validation sessions will provide SMEs with an opportunity to confirm that the workflows created and proposed for operations are a good fit for us. The final decisions made in these sessions will be reflected in the system build-out.
- **Who/Where:** Clinical/operational owners and SMEs will represent their departments during all rounds of Validation. While it is not possible to include every interested employee or clinician at each session, the Project Team has identified hundreds of SMEs to ensure there is representation from across the organization. Each person will be prepared to verify the design of the application alongside EHR systems staff.

Sessions will occur in meeting rooms across the organization. In early June, personalized schedules were sent to all SMEs for the first round of sessions from {NAME}. Personalized schedules will be sent out for Validation Rounds two, three, and four in advance as they are developed. There will also be SME "validation education" meetings set up during the month of July. The following Validation dates are final:

As always, please email {NAME} with any questions, comments, or feedback.

**Example Communication 3.4: Executive Memo
to All Leaders Calling for SME Nominations**

Title: Subject Matter Expert Nominations
Mode of Communication: Email
Target Audience: Managers and above
Sent from: CMIO/ Project Director
To: All Leaders

We are at a point in the pre-implementation process where we are engaging members of our community for their knowledge and expertise. Specifically, we are looking for subject matter experts (SMEs) – individuals who are proficient in operational process and policy for their given area, department, or workflow. Over the next several weeks, the Project Team will identify hundreds of SMEs from across the institution in one of the following ways:

- The Project Team will contact an individual directly based on knowledge of that person's expertise.
- Managers may recommend a team member for consideration.
- Individuals may volunteer by contacting their manager.

This week we will send an email to the entire community introducing the SME role. The email will outline the three ways that the Project Team will compile the SME list. For those individuals who are interested in volunteering, we will ask that they discuss the commitment with their manager. During those conversations, we advise that you use the below details about the SME role to provide clarity and expectations to your staff. Once those conversations are complete, please submit your vetted list of recommended names to **Product Director {NAME}** no later than **{DATE}**. We will only accept SME recommendations from managers.

About the SME Role

SMEs will work closely with the Project Team leading up to and during Kickoff, Discovery, and Validation. SMEs will continue to support throughout the lifecycle of the project to ensure we are building the system to meet our needs. Their responsibilities will be to make decisions regarding the new system's configuration, content, and workflows. In addition, these individuals will help us uphold our guiding principles by serving as decision makers, change agents, and communicators throughout the duration of the project.

SMEs Require the Following Qualifications:

- A willingness to be a participant for the duration of the project, or at least two years. This will include regular meetings with the Project Team and participation in larger project initiatives. Specific details

about additional meeting dates and times will be communicated to the
final SMEs once the identification process is complete in late April
- Foundational knowledge of processes and policies within their area
- The ability to speak to current successes and improvement opportunities in their areas to support the Project Team in implementing the system
- The ability to represent **{ORGANIZATION}** and the integrated needs of the organization
- The ability to communicate back to the department/end-user community as an extension of the Project Team
- An excitement about the project and the transformation ahead

 As the project progresses and we learn more about our needs,
we may solicit your help again to find additional SMEs. We
appreciate your support and leadership in this effort.

Example Communication 3.5: Invitation to Validation Sessions

Title: Validation Session Invitation
Mode of Communication: Email
Target Audience: All SMEs
Sent from: Project Team

Earlier this month, you received your schedule for the first
round of Validation sessions.

By now you should have RSVP'd to the sessions you can attend. For the
sessions you are unable to attend, please identify the appropriate individual
to represent your role, if you have not done so already. If you have not
received a link to your schedule, that means your attendance is not required
for this first round of Validation sessions.

We are continuing to prepare schedules for the next rounds of Validation
sessions in August and September, and are working to get those distributed
as soon as possible.

Our next priority is to ensure that you walk into your first Validation session prepared and ready to contribute. All SMEs are invited to attend one
Validation preparation meeting, which will serve as your education on all
things Validation-related. The Project Team will host individual meetings in
the morning and afternoon during these 3 days to accommodate as many
schedules as possible. Additionally, there will be a bridge line available if
you are unable to physically attend. *You only need to attend one of the 15
sessions.*

Please review the schedule and use the RSVP capability to enroll in one
of the available times. We'd like to reiterate that Validation is a critical step

for those workflow decisions that will be incorporated into the system build.

We want to hear your input, so your attendance and participation is essential. In alignment with our guiding principles, decisions are made by those who show up. Thanks again for your support and we look forward to seeing you at Validation prep!

Example Communication 3.6: Post-Validation Session Survey

Title: Post-Validation Session Survey
Mode of Communication: Email
Target Audience: All SMEs
Sent from: Project Team

Key Takeaways:

- The successful completion of Validation Session 2 means we are 50 percent complete with this phase of the project; Validation Session 3 and our final session, known as Re-engineering, is coming up. Schedules for September's sessions have been distributed and October schedules are forthcoming.
- Our team is working hard to refine each round of Validation to improve the experience. Please take a quick follow-up survey by **{DATE}** to let us know how we did. If this was the first round of Validation Sessions in which you have participated, please offer your feedback in the comments section of the survey.
- You are making a difference! Help share your experiences among your co-workers and colleagues with the below details and speaking points about Validation Session 2.
- As we wrap up this phase of the project, some of you will be asked to participate in Content Design Sessions, which will begin during the coming weeks. More information will be available soon.

Chapter 4

Engage and Train End Users

Everything you have done until this point in your implementation – visioning, planning, and engaging staff across your enterprise – has been leading to the organizational changes that will begin in this chapter. This transitional stage, which involves engagement, training, and preparation in the Communications and Change Leadership Model, is where the "rubber meets the road." Many organizations find this time to be one of the most challenging to help ensure their new EHR implementation sees long-term success. During this period, your entire enterprise should be involved with the project in some way, while multiple groups will be deeply engaged and should be leveraged to help provide support and facilitate change. The scope of your audiences and the importance of their engagement make this stage one of the most critical for robust and effective communications activities.

Training: End Users and Providers

Training for end users and providers will be one of the most important and broad-reaching activities you will encounter throughout your EHR implementation. Depending on the culture of your organization, it can also be one of the most difficult activities to effectively communicate and achieve user engagement around, due to the effort and time commitments that will be required. For this reason, it is important to use a variety of communications tools that align with the registration and training strategies your organization has chosen to pursue (Table 4.1 and Figure 4.1).

Table 4.1 In This Section

Activity/Event	Primary Objectives	Key Messaging Points	Communications Tools
4.1 Training: End Users and Providers	• Build a solid user base of staff and providers who are comfortable using the new EHR system.	• This process is a significant change for our entire enterprise and will take time. • Many have successfully gone before us to pave the way. We will be successful, just as they were. • Completing all training and practice requirements will help ensure we are ready and make the transition easier.	• Email updates: Training timeline, expectations by role • Intranet website: Resources, tools, and registration • Meeting roadshow: Overview of training program and time commitment specific to departments • Online learning tools: Access to online webinars and e-learning • Decentralized meetings: Operational leadership should reinforce informally through huddles and meetings directly with staff.
4.2 Training and Refreshers: Superusers and Supplemental At-The-Elbow Support	• Ensure adequate go-live support for end users during go-live and beyond. • Create positive "buzz" and staff excitement leading up to training.	• You are our end users' first line of support for questions and issues. • You are a positive, calming voice when others are unsure. • You are an agent of change. • You are empowered and encouraged to report any issues you encounter. • Your support is key to our success.	• Email updates • Intranet website: Dedicated superuser site with specific resources and tools • Superuser meeting: Led by operations, focus on superuser needs, preparation, and backfill

(Continued)

Table 4.1 (Continued) In This Section

Activity/Event	Primary Objectives	Key Messaging Points	Communications Tools
4.3 Training: Specialty Provider Trainers	• Offer specialty-focused training and support for providers. • Create peer-based champions to help address provider-specific questions and concerns.	• Some workflows are going to change, based on the insights and input we received from clinical and operational subject matter experts. • Time spent completing provider training greatly increases productivity during go-live. • Continued feedback from physicians is needed and encouraged	• Email updates: Targeted to specialty provider trainers • Intranet website: Resources and tools • General meeting: Overview of training program and time commitment specific to departments/providers • Decentralized meetings: Specific to provider specialty, review key training content, approach, timeline • Online learning tools: Access to online webinars and e-learning
4.4 Operations: Technical and Workflow Dress Rehearsals	• Ensure necessary technical components are in place and functioning properly prior to go-live. • Ensure subject matter experts, leaders, and staff are aware of key workflows that are changing, and prepare them to be ambassadors within their peer groups.	• Hardware strategies will change as part of the EHR implementation with the addition of shared workstations, new equipment, mobile devices, group printing, and more. • Some key workflows will change as we streamline processes, and implement new best practices to improve efficiency, patient safety, financial results, and other key performance metrics. • All users should educate themselves on how these changes will impact the way they conduct patient care and other operational functions.	• Email updates: Timeline and expectations • Intranet website: Resources, dates, video links • Meeting roadshow: Overview of technical deployments and system demos

(Continued)

Table 4.1 (Continued)   In This Section

Activity/Event	Primary Objectives	Key Messaging Points	Communications Tools
4.5 Operations: Go-Live Readiness and Preparations	• Inform and empower leaders and staff with specific information needed to successfully execute during go-live.	• In addition to the careful planning and preparations being done by the EHR Project Team, there are specific operational and business actions you will need to take prior to go-live.	• Email updates: Milestone timeline, go-live expectations • Intranet website: Resources and tools • Meeting roadshow: Overview of timeline, key events, and operational time commitment • Readiness checklist: Detailed monthly task list • Decentralized meetings: Operational leadership should reinforce informally through huddles and meetings directly with staff.

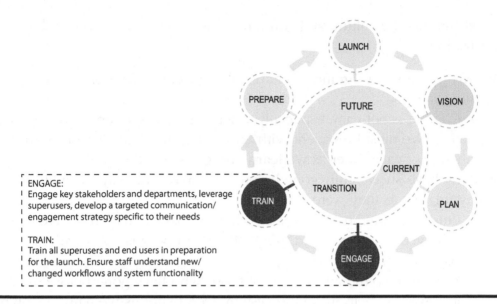

Figure 4.1   Engage and train.

Audience

Your communications strategy should engage virtually everyone across the enterprise at this time. The precise strategy for end users and providers will need to be crafted around how your training and registration process has been established.

- If end users and providers will self-register for training, you will want to use a multimodal communications approach and should create a plan that involves numerous reminders with an increasing sense of urgency. Consider employing a countdown mechanism, and continue actively pushing reminders out to those who haven't yet registered. You should set an earlier deadline than needed, so it can be extended in the event that additional time is required to complete training registration.
- If managers or supervisors will be responsible for registering their staff for training, you should have a list of those leaders with contact methods readily available, set clear deadlines for each step of the process, and provide regular status updates to ensure all end users are registered based on the established timelines.

Key Objectives and Message Points

The following message points will be important to use with end users and providers. Remember that messaging should always be framed within a context that fits the culture and communications strategy of your unique organization.

- This process is a significant change for our entire enterprise and will take time.
  - Change is not easy, especially when it involves an entire organization. We must be patient with each other and with ourselves, and support each other as we learn and grow together.
- Many have successfully gone before us to pave the way. We will be successful, just as they were.
  - Our organization – like many others across the nation – have carefully vetted and selected this EHR system because of its robust patient care functions.
  - We will reap the advantages of those who have gone before us, and we will help make the system even better as we gain our own knowledge of it and develop expertise.
- Completing all training and practice requirements will help ensure we are ready and will make the transition easier during go-live.
  - Training classes alone will not be sufficient to ensure we are prepared and confident using the new EHR system at go-live.
  - There is no substitute for practice! Practice will not make us perfect on "day one" – but it will make things significantly easier for everyone!

 Find ways to infuse excitement into training and other activities leading up to go-live! This is likely the first point during your project where virtually every staff member will become involved in some way. Celebrate that with an event, a message from the CEO, or other activity that best fits the culture of your organization. (See Example Communication 4.1)

Communications Tools

The following communications tools will be useful to reach and prepare end users and providers:

- Training classes
  - In-class training will likely be the primary method used to educate providers and users about the new EHR system. Keep in mind that

you might face resistance from some users, depending on the number of hours of training they are expected to complete.

■ Online learning
  - Many organizations will supplement in-class work with additional online training to reduce the number of classroom hours required.
■ Practice environment
  - A practice environment that mimics the functionality of your production environment will be extremely important to ensure end users have the opportunity to become more comfortable using the EHR system.
■ Hands-on sessions
  - Hands-on support sessions and demos are good opportunities for trainers and Project Team members to personally interact with users and alleviate confusion and concerns.
■ Knowledgebase
  - Your organization's knowledgebase will be a consistent source of reference materials (documentation, tip sheets, etc.) that you will need to utilize throughout training and go-live.
■ Intranet and online
  - Online sites are useful for providing deeper layers of communications detail that can't be contained within an email or other communication, as well as serving to archive important news and updates for future reference.
■ Email updates
  - Email updates are typically one of the most utilized and accessible means to reach staff and providers with important and timely messages.
  - Keep in mind that while email communications can be quick and easy, overuse of them can create communications fatigue and lead to people "turning off" your message completely.
■ Surveys
  - Bidirectional feedback will be critical during training (and any other transitional phase) to help gather input directly from users about their experiences. The facts you gather should then be used to adjust strategies and inform future messaging points.
■ Printed materials (i.e., pocket guides, quick reference cards)
  - Quick printed references can be a short-term solution that is quick and easily accessible for staff in the clinical environment.

■ Videos
  – Videos are a good way to engage staff and get people excited. They should be short (60–90 seconds) and used sparingly. Keep in mind that videos, especially if professionally produced, can require a high investment of time and money and result in relatively low returns. Therefore, if you are going to make the investment, you should have a purposeful plan to use the video – at the beginning of each training class, for example (See Example Communication 4.1).
■ Countdown clocks
  – These serve as subtle reminders that go-live is approaching and help raise the sense of urgency to prepare (See Figure 4.2)!

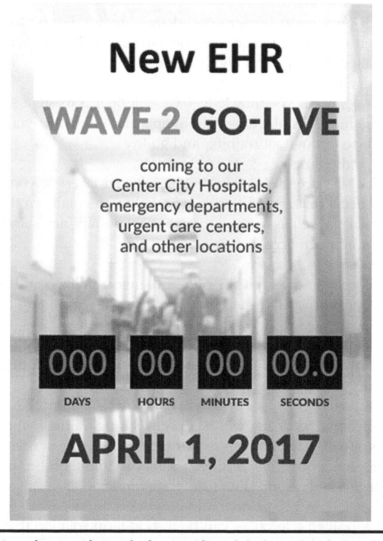

Figure 4.2   Sample countdown clock poster board design. Digital countdown clocks can be found online and affixed to the boards.

Example Communication 4.1: Executive Introduction to Training Video Script

Title: Executive Introduction to Training
Mode of Communication: Pre-recorded Video for Classroom Training
Target Audience: All Staff

Your CEO/Executive:

Hello, and welcome to training! I wanted to take a few moments to remind you how special this time is and thank you for your commitment and participation. As you know, innovation is at the heart of our vision and values, and this transformation will better prepare us to shape and innovate the future of exceptional healthcare here.

Same/Other Leader:

Whether you are a fellow physician, a provider, superuser, leader or valued member of our support staff, we all have one thing in common – we are now "end users" for our new EHR system. That means we all have a shared responsibility to take in everything we can during training. This transition will only occur once, and it is up to each of us to make the experience valuable and ensure our transformation is as meaningful as possible.

Same/Other Leader:

We recognize that training involves a significant investment of your time and efforts. That's on top of the countless hours many of you have already put in to help validate, build, and test our new workflows. Know that your investments are valued and appreciated – and, above all, they are what will make us successful in the long run. Every productive hour we invest now will result in days of productivity and efficiency during the months and years to come. What you are doing now will truly transform the future of health care for you, your fellow caregivers, and most importantly – our patients.

Your CEO/Executive:

So now that you're focused on why training is so important, I want to remind you of one more thing – let's have fun! Change isn't always easy, but this is an exciting time for our organization, and you are the most important part of this journey. So buckle into your seats, make sure your tray tables are raised, and get ready for training. The next stop is go-live!

Make your video (and any other engagement activities) as fun, exciting, and "out of the box" as you like, based on your organization's culture and/or the theme of your EHR implementation. Sometimes, doing the unexpected or approaching things in a new way is what gets your staff engaged!

Training and Refreshers: Superusers and Supplemental At-The-Elbow Support

Initial training and "refresher" training for superusers and support staff will be critical to the long-term success of your transition. It is best to have a Project Team leader to serve as a coordinator for your superusers, and that person should work closely with the Communications Team to coordinate the timing of activities and messages.

Audience

Within most organizations, superusers will consist of employees who are selected or recruited for support. This approach helps reduce the overall costs associated with supporting go-live, and it also simplifies the sharing of information throughout operational readiness preparations and go-live, since employees will typically have direct access to email, intranet, and other tools used for internal communications.

Because supplemental "at-the-elbow" resources may be secured and managed through a third party, be sure your vendor is engaged and has a coordinator embedded within the Project Team for consistent messaging and the strategic execution of communications. Work with your vendor to identify and understand the communications channels and methods available to reach supplemental support staff. Often you will need to use different communications channels than those for superusers since contracted support staff will only be engaged for a period of weeks around go-live.

Key Objectives and Message Points

You are the end users' first line of support. Be sure to re-emphasize why your end users were selected to support their peers:

- Reputation as a "go-to" person
- Respect they have among their peers

■ Expertise in their area
■ Positive attitude
■ Receptiveness to change

You are a positive, calming voice when others are unsure. Be sure superusers are prepared to reassure end users with confidence – understanding the support resources that are available, including:

■ Command center
■ Leadership rounders
■ Trainers
■ Regular updates and communications
■ Self-help resources (i.e., tip sheets, knowledgebase, system tooltips, etc.)

You are an agent of change. Provide sample talking points for superusers to share when change is difficult:

■ Everyone (even superusers) won't be completely comfortable on day one, no matter how much training or practice they have completed. That's okay – it's a natural part of the process!
■ It's normal for the period around training and go-live to feel hectic and disruptive, no matter how well things have been prepared.
■ This is a transformational time for our organization – it won't be easy or perfect, but the results of our work will create positive results for everyone involved.
■ We will get through these changes successfully while providing excellent care as long as we work together and continue to focus on our patients.

You are empowered and encouraged to report any issues. Be sure to share the following reminders with superusers:

■ Leverage your training knowledge and experience to resolve problems at-the-elbow first, whenever possible.
■ Know and understand the process for reporting and escalating issues, when needed.
■ Be sure to report any issues that you or end users encounter.
■ Reassure end users that their problems are being addressed as quickly as possible, based on priority.

Don't assume someone else has already reported a problem. Don't create workarounds for problems or allow others to do so. Doing so exacerbates problems, delays solutions, and makes root cause analyses more difficult.

Your support will be essential for success. Superusers and supplemental support staff will become the face of change during this time. Remind them that it is important to:

■ Acknowledge when things go wrong
■ Move through difficult moments while maintaining a positive attitude
■ Be a "cheerleader" and find ways to celebrate the small things that are being done right!

Communications/Engagement Tools

In addition to the communication and engagement tools listed at the beginning of this chapter, the following tools will be useful to prepare superusers and at-the-elbow support:

■ Training classes
    – In-class training will likely be the primary method used to educate superusers. Do your best to keep them excited and engaged about their role during this time.
■ Surveys
    – Bidirectional feedback will be critical during training (and any other transitional phase) to help gather input directly from superusers about their experiences. The facts you gather should then be used to adjust strategies and inform future messaging for other groups.
■ Refresher meetings
    – Refresher meetings and training are most important for superusers since they typically kick off their roles and receive training

earlier than end users. This means there can be a significant gap between early activities and go-live. Holding refreshers shortly before go-live is a good way to remind superusers about their roles and responsibilities and why they were chosen in the first place.

■ Contests and rewards
   – A structured rewards program for superusers can be a great way to generate engagement and encourage them to interact and maintain their momentum as they learn and grow together (See S.U.P.E.R. Program sample resources).

Key Considerations and Lessons Learned

Identifying large numbers of superusers with operational and clinical support is a detailed and lengthy process, so it will be important to start early. Be aware that the long timeline means there can be an extended gap between your first engagement of superusers (i.e., selection, kickoff meetings, etc.) and training and go-live. Consider the following strategies to keep this important group engaged:

■ Provide pre-learning opportunities prior to formal training activities. Your EHR vendor should offer online resources and other documentation that can be used as a basis.
■ Create a structured rewards program with a hierarchy of achievements, and provide tangible and visible rewards as superusers reach higher levels (See Figure 4.3). Doing so will:
   – Incentivize superusers to participate and engage frequently
   – Help superusers become more familiar with the new EHR, so their training will be more effective
   – Track superuser knowledge and development to ensure you are positioned for successful support during go-live
■ Plan ahead to ensure the practice environment and basic training materials are ready for communication so superusers can leverage after training.

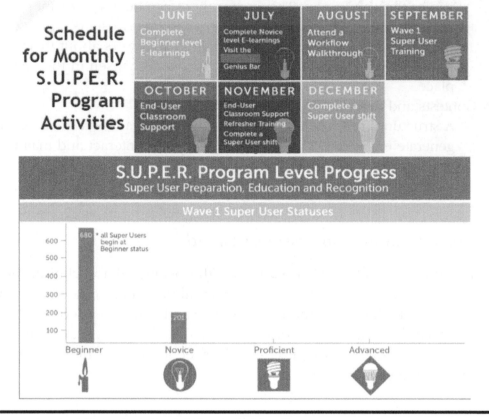

Figure 4.3   Sample activities calendar and rewards program structure for superusers.

Training: Specialty Provider Trainers

Specialty provider trainers (SPTs) will be an important resource for their physician and provider peers throughout end-user training and go-live-focused training and support for providers. Remember to include them when you create communications for superusers and supplemental at-the-elbow support.

Audience

Each clinical specialty usually identifies at least one provider that will train as an SPT, someone who will be responsible for helping to train their peers on new specialty-specific workflows in the EHR system. These individuals are typically well-respected among their peers, influencers within the clinical enterprise, and positioned to help serve as ambassadors among other physician leadership groups.

Key Objectives and Message Points

You will want to provide SPTs with some basic messages they can use when talking and working with their peers. The following are important points to emphasize:

- Some workflows are going to change based on the insights and input we received from clinical and operational subject matter experts. Whenever possible, efforts are being made to streamline and standardize workflows and eliminate unnecessary steps for providers.
- Time spent completing provider training will greatly increase our productivity during go-live. By offering specialty-specific training, we will be able to optimize general training time and potentially decrease in-class time for providers. Specialty training results in a more highly specialized training experience, greater expertise using the system, and quicker stabilization after go-live.
- Continued feedback from physicians and providers is needed and encouraged. Training and go-live are not the end – they are only the beginning of the process to continue enhancing and optimizing our new EHR system.

Key Considerations and Lessons Learned

- Clearly outline the expectation and commitment of time that will be involved for specialty provider training.
- Be sure SPTs and their peers understand the specific topics that they will be covering and will be expected to understand and support.
- Communicate training times as early as possible – 4–8 weeks in advance or more is not too early, since clinical and provider schedules are often completed months in advance.

Operations: Technical and Workflow Dress Rehearsals

Audience

Managers, department leaders, subject matter experts, and other key operational staff should be engaged in "dress rehearsals" to help ensure they understand and are ready for the changes that will occur during and after go-live.

Key Objectives and Message Points

■ Hardware strategies will change as part of the EHR implementation with the addition of shared workstations, new equipment, mobile devices, group printing, and more.

■ Some key workflows will change as we streamline processes, and implement new best practices to improve efficiency, patient safety, financial results, and other key performance metrics.

■ All users should educate themselves on how these changes will impact the way they conduct patient care and other operational functions.

Communications Tools

■ Email updates
  – Email updates are typically one of the most utilized and accessible means to reach leadership and subject matter experts with important and timely messages.
  – Keep in mind that while email communications can be quick and easy, overuse of them can create communications fatigue and lead to people "turning off" your message completely.

■ Meetings and in-person "dress rehearsal" group sessions
  – In order to effectively demonstrate new workflows, group sessions will be helpful. They also serve as a good opportunity to provide immediate feedback from leaders, so you can get a sense of how end users might react to the workflow and other changes.

Key Considerations and Lessons Learned

■ Dress rehearsals are often conducted in a large auditorium setting. Plan ahead to ensure the logistics are handled and necessary space is available, especially since meeting spaces, conference rooms, and other group areas will be at a premium during training and go-live.

■ Aside from workflow changes, one of the most significant impacts on users will be changes to hardware and how they use it. You will need to address changes to any of the following items:
  – Desktop computers, laptops, thin client/virtual machines, monitors, etc.

– Mobile workstations, computers on wheels, built-in clinical workstations, etc.
– Printers, scanners, multifunction devices, etc.
  • Be on the lookout for changes that seem "small" but have broad-reaching impacts or consequences. Configuration changes as simple as prescription paper moving to a different drawer in a copier or printer can cause significant issues if users are not aware that they need to change their behavior.
– Tablets, smartphones, mobile devices, etc.
  • If your new EHR offers applications for mobile devices, be prepared to explain those features and outline the step-by-step process end users will need to follow to install and use the applications on their devices.
– Dictation stations, microphones, cameras, etc.

Chapter 5

Prepare for Launch: Technical and Operational Readiness

Operational readiness should remain a key focal point throughout your electronic health record (EHR) implementation. A newly configured EHR with deployed and tested technology and hardware will likely function as designed, but if end users are ill-equipped to utilize the tools and manage their workflows, that well-designed system will still come to a halt. Preparation is vital. Table 5.1 outlines the key topics and messages that should be delivered as you begin preparing your staff and users for go-live (Figure 5.1).

Pre Go-Live Changes

You should expect that your new EHR will present a significant departure from current state workflows. Fortunately, there are often a variety of operational changes that can be made in advance of your go-live. Doing so can prove highly effective, since changing workflows and processes in the legacy system (when possible) will allow additional time for staff to adjust to any changes or new responsibilities. Then, at go-live, the emphasis for staff can be placed on using the new EHR instead of learning a new EHR and new workflows at once. Whenever possible, you should consider systematic, incremental changes to help reduce the impacts on staff.

Table 5.1 In This Section

Activity/Event	Primary Objectives	Key Messaging Points	Communications Tools
5.1 Pre Go-Live Changes	• Emphasis on key operational workflow changes that can be made prior to go-live. This reduces the level of change that will occur on the day of go-live.	• It is easier to change workflows and processes before the EHR launch; there is less for staff to learn and adjust to during go-live. • Standardizing workflows across departments will ensure smooth flow and simplify the system.	• Email updates: Messaging on key strategies and targeted workflows • Decentralized meetings: Led by operations, departmental/workgroup meetings to review and address identified workflows
5.2 Operational Readiness	• Key tasks, responsibilities, and considerations that operational stakeholders need to address leading up to go-live. Some deliverables may need significant lead time to ensure adequate staffing, coverage, and support.	• What does "ready for go-live" look like and mean? • How can you ensure a successful transition to the new EHR and limit business/clinical operations disruptions?	• Email updates: Timeline and important updates • Readiness Checklist: Detailed list of tasks to be completed leading up to go-live • Monthly roadshow presentations: Updates on operational readiness including focused review of at-risk departments and end-user groups • Decentralized meetings: Led by operations, departmental/workgroup meetings to review and address readiness checklist items

(Continued)

Table 5.1 (Continued) In This Section

Activity/Event	Primary Objectives	Key Messaging Points	Communications Tools
5.3 Individual Readiness	• Similar to above, define the considerations and responsibilities that each individual has as it pertains to preparedness and engagement.	• What does "ready for go-live" look like and mean from an individual's perspective? • Leverage the training playground to practice – practice is the key to a smooth go-live. • Understand how to report issues and where to find resources to help. • Know who your superusers are and when they will be staffed.	• Email updates: Timeline and important updates • Readiness checklist: Detailed list of tasks to be completed leading up to go-live, including individual responsibilities • Monthly roadshow presentations: Updates on operational readiness including focused review of at-risk departments and end-user groups • Decentralized meetings: Led by operations, departmental/workgroup meetings to review and address readiness checklist items specific to end-user groups • Online playground: Training tools to enable staff to practice
5.4 System Demos and Simulations	• Demonstrations of the new EHR workflows, features, and functionalities – highlighting key benefits and potential risk areas that inform operational readiness.	• Understand the main similarities and differences between the old and new EHR. • What features or functions in the new EHR require additional training or operational planning to ensure smooth workflows? • What scenarios/ workflows are high-risk and what plans need to be in place to mitigate potential problems?	• Demonstrations in large/small forums: Review of common workflows to show broader integration of new EHR • Video-recorded sessions: For those unable to attend in person, online reference tool to demos • Facilitated simulations: Focused scenarios/workflows that represent new and/or high-risk changes with the EHR

(Continued)

Table 5.1 (Continued)   In This Section

Activity/Event	Primary Objectives	Key Messaging Points	Communications Tools
5.5 Go-Live Logistics	• Specific preparations and expectations for the EHR go-live including technical support strategies, issue resolution, and end-user at-the-elbow support, among others. Also includes details specific to the transition of legacy systems to the new EHR, including tasks and responsibilities as well as what data/ information to expect in the new system.	• Specific dates, times, and events leading up to and through go-live. • Contact information and ticket resolution process details. • Where to find key legacy data that was not converted to the new EHR. • Where to find updates on go-live activities and major system issues.	• Email updates: Timeline and important updates • Readiness checklist: Detailed list of tasks to be completed leading up to go-live • Monthly roadshow presentations: Updates on logistics including super-user staffing, technical deployments, and IT support plans • Decentralized meetings: Led by operations, departmental/workgroup meetings to review and address readiness checklist items specific to end-user groups
5.6 Final Preparation/ Motivation	• Message from the CEO to motivate staff and ensure heightened readiness.	• We can accomplish anything as a team. • Thank the organization for the tremendous amount of effort and time commitment to prepare as well as the effort required during/through the go-live.	• Email/ video: Personal opportunity for CEO to share thoughts and encouragement broadly

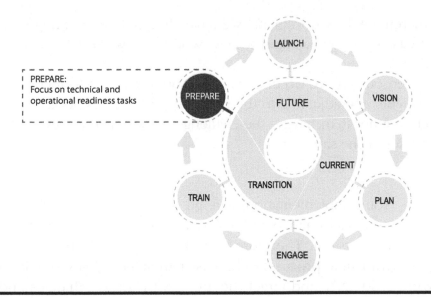

Figure 5.1   Prepare.

Audience

Pre go-live communications should involve all stakeholders who will be impacted by the new EHR implementation. Keep in mind that departments or end-user groups that will experience significant workflow changes leading up to or during go-live will require additional support and information to assist with those transitions. During this time, the operational leaders that you developed strong relationships with earlier in the project will serve a prominent role in making decisions and aligning resources in the face of competing priorities.

Key Objectives and Message Points

The following message points will be important to use during this phase:

■ Workflow and process changes that can occur before go-live will make the transition smoother and allow you to focus on incremental change.
  – Adapting to new workflows and processes with a new EHR will be challenging and potentially overwhelming.
  – We are working to limit the impact of significant changes and, when necessary, break them down to make them more manageable for users.

- Incremental improvements we have already been making will make it easier for you to adjust to new workflows when our EHR system is live.
- When our go-live occurs, we want you to be able to focus on your patients and adjusting to the new system (features, look and feel, etc.) rather than having the challenge of performing new responsibilities at the same time.

 Your implementation will go smoother if departments/end users can change and adopt new workflows within their current system. The more time they have to develop familiarity with new processes, the easier their new EHR system adoption will be. Identify and target the areas with drastic changes and significant workflows variations (current state compared to the new EHR future state).

Communications Tools

The following communications tools will be useful to prepare departments:

- ■ Email/Website
  - Provide regular updates and resources to inform and direct leaders and key stakeholders through the pre go-live changes.
  - When possible, use stories and examples from other organizations. Infusing your updates with a human interest component will result in greater interest and staff engagement.
- ■ Roadshow presentations
  - Conduct monthly roadshow presentations for management teams and specific departments, highlighting specific workflow and process changes that will be made during this phase.
  - Emphasize the importance of stakeholder involvement, end-user engagement, and preparation, as well as resource needs, which will become greater during this time.
- ■ Operational workgroup meetings
  - Using your targeted workflows and processes, assemble your subject matter experts (SMEs) and key stakeholders into a formal workgroup. That group should have input for any plans to move from

current to future state, including training, support, and oversight needs.

– These groups should meet on a regular basis (e.g., weekly or biweekly) to ensure decisions continue moving and action plans can be implemented on schedule.

The following is a sample email that can be sent to your staff and end-user community articulating the importance of pre go-live changes. While many changes will be specific to departments or end-user groups (e.g., pharmacy, lab, physicians, critical care nurse, etc.), the general message can be applied across all areas of your enterprise.

Example Communication 5.1: Pre Go-Live Changes

Title: Pre Go-Live Changes
Mode of Communication: Email
Target Audience: All Staff
Sent from: CMIO

Taking Action Now to Ensure Smooth Implementation

In a recent memo, Project Team leadership described the benefit of making workflow/process improvements now, in advance of Go-Live. To accomplish this, we need a plan to evolve from our current, fragmented state of electronic health information, to the new future of a single, integrated electronic health record. They explained that we are identifying actions *now* that will ease our transition *later* and ultimately enable our long-term implementation to be smooth and streamlined.

More from Their Letter to Staff

One example of how we are operationalizing this approach today is through the rollout of Structured Note and Charge Capture. We are beginning to plan for this implementation with each clinical practice so that over the next 2 years, every department can familiarize themselves with the design and functionality of the new EHR note functionality.

In the coming weeks, we will share information about another initiative that will systematically collect information about a patient's "care team," consisting of their primary and specialist care providers. Doing this will ensure we improve the effectiveness of our communications across the care continuum.

Another way we can adopt this approach is to allocate resources and standardize processes now. We need to ensure that our staff – including our medical assistants (MAs) and nurses – are effectively documenting through our electronic system at the "top of their license." This will help us further streamline the patient care experience.

The Project Team will also provide prime opportunities for us to rethink the design of our current workflows before new workflows are implemented in 2 years.

These are just some of the ways we are taking a proactive stance to better prepare ourselves for the rapid and efficient adoption of the new system – well in advance of Go-Live.

Operational Readiness

As your organization nears go-live, it will be important to confirm that you are operationally ready at the local and departmental levels across the enterprise to ensure success. This will involve close communications with leadership and a high level of engagement from operations. Depending on the scope and complexity of your EHR implementation, your operational readiness program may be straightforward or quite robust. Regardless of the complexity, you should have a clear strategy, operational sponsorship, and staff engagement from all impacted areas.

Additionally, your EHR project should have a defined operational readiness leader responsible for overseeing the key tasks and progress of each area. Typically, an internal leader or other champion will be best suited for that role, since they will understand the organizational culture, can navigate politics and decision making, should have a clinical background or strong operational knowledge, and will be viewed as a key influencer for change. Of course, you must also be sure to select someone who has the bandwidth to prioritize their time for this effort. Figure 5.2 provides a sample structure for the inpatient operational readiness program.

Operational readiness will require a carefully planned and well-defined structure to successfully prepare for change and drive results. The following is a recommended approach:

- ■ Structure:
  - – Biweekly meetings to review operational readiness.
- ■ Process:
  - – Conducted by operational leadership.
  - – Agenda should include detailed reviews of high-volume, high-risk, and net new workflows; error queues and work queues; and cross-walking your organization's overall current state to future state.
  - – Reviews should be completed and signed off by department administrators.

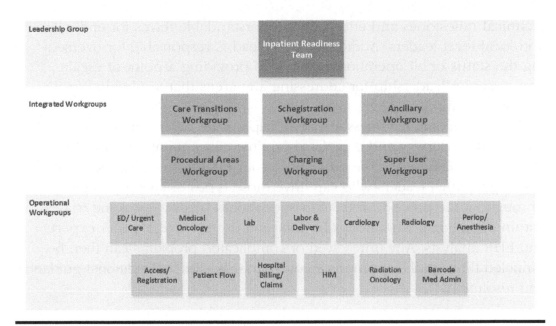

Figure 5.2 Inpatient operational readiness structure.

- – Subsequent sessions should become increasingly focused on details and can be facilitated jointly by operations and your EHR team to reinforce key workflows and expectations.
- – Ongoing: Operational readiness workflows and work queues should become agenda items for the weekly operational workgroup meetings.
- ■ Outcomes:
  - – Document the completion of workflow and work queue reviews.
  - – Assign operational managers with next steps for operational readiness based on the review process.
  - – Verify and sign off for all completed tasks.
  - – Participants: Leadership – from C-level to directors, managers, and supervisors – will need to be engaged to ensure the proper steps are taken in preparation for go-live.
  - – Workflow and work queue review: Department administrators and operational managers.
  - – Sign-off: Operational readiness lead, EHR project leadership.

Operational Readiness Lead

The operational readiness lead(s) will serve as the bridge between the EHR team and key operational areas. That person should help translate technical milestones and efforts into understandable terms for end users and local level leaders. Additionally, the lead is responsible for overseeing the status of all operational areas and providing a point of escalation to senior leadership for addressing any areas that are behind or underperforming.

The operational readiness lead will help ensure organizational preparations are underway and completed on time. Since many operational changes will fall outside the purview of your EHR team, it will be helpful to have operational leaders who can drive those types of changes in parallel. Throughout the process, risks and issues should be discussed and triaged within operational workgroups by your end users, subject matter experts, and EHR analysts. Any unresolved or complicated problems can then be funneled through the appropriate governance bodies for additional guidance and resolution.

Integrated Workgroups

Integrated workgroups represent horizontal, cross-functional departments or areas that do not reside under a single department or leader. Those groups should identify and help resolve any cross-functional processes that might present challenges or be difficult to manage in your new EHR system (Table 5.2).

Operational Workgroups

Figure 5.2 highlights the core operational workgroups that will be made up of operational subject matter experts and EHR analysts. Those groups should collaborate throughout your EHR implementation – from system configuration, build and testing, through training and go-live. Depending on the scope of your project, you might also need to consider additional workgroups for specific areas such as:

- Case Management
- Oncology
- Therapies – Physical Therapy (PT), Occupational Therapy (OT), Respiratory
- Infection Control
- Quality and Safety

Table 5.2 Integrated Workgroups

Workgroup Name	Purpose
Care Transitions	Evaluate communication and processes for patients that change level of service (i.e., settings, units, etc.). Include emphasis for inpatient (IP) to outpatient (OP).
Schegistration	Evaluate communication and processes for scheduling, registration, and other related activities across all settings/locations.
Ancillary	Evaluate communication and processes related to radiology, lab, and other ancillary diagnostic settings and the sending/receiving areas.
Superuser	Develop and oversee strategy execution for superuser education, engagement, and backfill.
Charging	Evaluate charging processes/methodologies across departments and disciplines.
Procedural Areas	Evaluate communication and processes for scheduling, care delivery, transfers, and other related activities across all settings/locations for procedural areas such as endo, bronc, etc.
Ambulatory Workgroup	Evaluate workflows and considerations across the ambulatory setting, including the patient portal, scheduling, outpatient clinical workflows, billing, referrals, and follow-ups.

- Nutrition and Dietetics
- Supply Chain and Materials Management
- Finance and General Ledger

The agenda in Table 5.3 provides a sample outline for operational readiness meetings. The content includes go-live logistics, Project Team updates, and EHR system and workflow reviews to reinforce key changes and identify areas that require additional discussion or support. Section 4 of the agenda – EHR System Review – provides a look ahead to future topics based on timing and your proximity to go-live. As your go-live date approaches, the focus of these meetings should shift toward operational readiness and the evaluation of any areas that are at risk or behind in preparations.

The following sample communication highlights content, deliverables, and expectations for revenue cycle and clinical leaders.

Table 5.3 Example Agenda for Operational Readiness Meeting

#	Topics	Time (Minutes)
1	Meeting Kickoff	3
2	Go-Live Logistics Update • Review of upcoming or past due action items tied to go-live • Logistics checklist (staffing/backfill, training, superusers, schedule conversions, etc.)	5
3	Project Team Updates • Review of milestones, outstanding tasks/decisions, and other upcoming tasks for: – Training (enrollment, completion, other updates) – Clinical operations – Access and revenue cycle – Reporting – Others as needed: technical, ancillary	20
4	New EHR System Review • Review of key workflows/work queues	30

	Meeting Date	Topic
	9/30	Schegistration • Process of making appointments • Check-in and ensure registration warnings/errors/ hard stops/workflow stops • Registration sidebar and how to use it
	10/7	Go-Live tasks • Training requirements • Superuser support • Command center/ help desk/ at-the-elbow support overview
	10/14	Charging • Charge trigger • Follow up with providers on close encounters • Charge reconciliation • Provider dashboard • RVUs

(Continued)

Table 5.3 (Continued)   Example Agenda for Operational Readiness Meeting

#	Topics	Time (Minutes)
	10/21 Edits • Charge edits • Coding edits • Scrubber edits • How to use work queue monitoring reports • Practice manager dashboard	
	10/28 Reporting • Physician charges/payments/adjustments • Overall practice revenue reporting • Overall practice scheduling reporting • Overall practice quality reporting	
	11/4 Go-Live Planning/Operational Readiness • Scenario reviews for access and revenue cycle processes • Common pitfalls and risks	
	11/11 Go-Live Planning/Operational Readiness • Scenario reviews for clinical operations processes • Common pitfalls and risks	
	11/18 Go-Live Planning/Operational Readiness • Final preparation and logistics review	
5	Ambulatory Practice Updates • Updates from practice administrators/managers related to operational readiness and go-live logistics	20
6	Recap of Follow-Up Action Items and Meeting Close • Topics or special guests for next meeting • Confirm actions and assignments	5

Example Communication 5.2: Readiness Details

Title: Revenue Cycle and Clinical Operations Readiness
Mode of Communication: Email
Target Audience: All Staff
Sent from: Project Team

Spotlight on Revenue Cycle Readiness

Because the new EHR is an integrated electronic health record (meaning its individual applications work seamlessly together as part of the overall system), it will bring significant improvements across the enterprise. At the same time, numerous teams and workgroups will help prepare for long-term success.

Revenue Cycle Preparation

Similar to Validation Sessions for workflows, the Revenue Cycle Preparedness team will bring operational experts into the design and decision-making process. In the current environment, Admissions, Scheduling, Health Information Management, Hospital Billing, Professional Billing (for medical offices), Case Management, Transport, and the Patient Flow Management Center use electronic systems that do not share data seamlessly. The new EHR will:

- Ensure that information from current systems is integrated
- Enable seamless data sharing between these and other departments
- Certify that Parallel Revenue Cycle Testing is completed
- Guarantee that claims are generated correctly (and will result in payment)

The team will also help organizational leadership identify and prepare for any operational changes associated with the new EHR and assist with educating staff members about business-related tools that will be available after Go-Live.

What Benefits Will Come from These Revenue Cycle Activities?

The program has a track record of success following Go-Lives, including:

- Significant reductions in accounts receivable days – or the number of days between delivery of care and payment
- Appropriate increases in average daily charges, cumulative payments, and revenues

Importantly, the program will also offer aggregated data from other institutions to help generate predictions for fluctuations in Access and Revenue Cycle metrics.

When Does the Team Meet?

The team meets biweekly to discuss issues and provide updates and status reports. Individual members of the team also meet with the Project Team analysts on an ongoing basis to help make decisions about how to build each Revenue Cycle application.

Spotlight on Clinical Operational Readiness

Because the EHR is an integrated electronic health record (meaning its individual applications work seamlessly together as part of the overall system), it will bring significant improvements across the enterprise. At the same time, numerous teams and workgroups – including Clinical Operational Readiness – will help prepare for long-term success.

This team will oversee the process of planning, selecting, designing, and building clinical content. Content refers to any details in the system that will support how end users will use a specific function – for example, a vitals flow sheet, order set, medication, etc.

Many clinical staff members will be involved in working sessions – including physicians, nurses, pharmacists, and other caregivers. Those subject matter experts will be responsible for attending sessions, making decisions, and representing their areas of specialty while thinking critically about any gaps. This work will help ensure the system functions efficiently and effectively.

When Do the Workgroups Meet?

All clinical application teams are involved in these workgroups, including Ambulatory, Ancillary, and Inpatient. Many of the same SMEs who contributed to Validation Sessions will also be involved in this process. The Project Team is evaluating content on an ongoing basis, and groups will meet during the coming weeks and months to continue reviewing that content.

Operational Readiness Checklist

One of the most influential and critical drivers of success during your EHR implementation will be the use of an operational readiness checklist. The checklist is a tool that outlines in detail what operational leaders and their staff need to accomplish at local levels of your organization in order to be ready for go-live. Table 5.4 provides a sample of a 3-month operational checklist. Each month, you will see a list of discrete actions that need to be reviewed and addressed. Follow-ups should be assigned by role for clear ownership by managers, providers, staff, superusers, subject matter experts, or operational readiness leads. Additionally, the tasks are accompanied by details and an estimated level of effort. This information will help your operational leaders plan and assign resources accordingly to ensure all tasks are completed on time.

Table 5.4 Operational Readiness Checklist

Dept. Roles Assigned to Task						
Manager	Providers	Staff	Superusers	SMEs, Op Readiness Lead	Action Required	The following deliverables/tasks should be complete by the months indicated below:	Level of Effort
End of April						
During the month of April, you will be working on tasks associated with preparedness for training and Go-Live support. At the end of the month, you will have a plan for managing staff backfill (if deemed necessary) during training and go-live periods. Additionally, for specialties you manage or are a part of, you will identify specialty provider trainers. It is best practice to have specialists trained by their peers. Over the next few months, the specialist trainer will work with the training team to refine the curriculum, set the training calendar, and provide additional decisions on the best way to optimize in-room training experiences for the specific specialty.						
X					Complete a key operational milestone.	Plan your backfill strategy for training and go-live support.	High
			X		Complete a key operational milestone.	Make sure your superusers attend kickoff meeting.	Low
X	X				Complete an important activity.	By April 15, identify specialty provider trainers who will be responsible for training all providers in their area.	Medium

(Continued)

Table 5.4 (Continued) Operational Readiness Checklist

Manager	Providers	Staff	Superusers	SMEs, Op Readiness Lead	Action Required	The following deliverables/tasks should be complete by the months indicated below:	Level of Effort
X				X	Complete a key operational milestone.	Identify the work queues your department owns and understand how these work queues fit into the larger work queue ownership structure. Ownership sign-off on all work queues – owning area, supervisors, managers, revenue cycle sponsor, executive sponsor.	High
X				X	Communicate effectively.	Present new EHR content/updates as a standing agenda item in your monthly staff meetings (at a minimum) using monthly talking points and roadshow slides for March.	Low

(Continued)

Table 5.4 (Continued)   Operational Readiness Checklist

Manager	Providers	Staff	Superusers	SMEs, Op Readiness Lead	Action Required	The following deliverables/tasks should be complete by the months indicated below:	Level of Effort
End of May							
						The month of May has several deliverables tied to staff scheduling. These include finalizing superuser training schedules/backfill/paid time off (PTO) strategies, and determining needs for pre go-live activities such as data conversion and abstraction, which cover both the electronic and manual population of data from existing systems into the new EHR. The Project Team will provide specific details on the various deliverables through SME workgroup meetings. Specialty content build will be signed off this month in advance of system testing by the Project Team.	
X					Complete an important activity.	Submit your superuser schedule and backfill strategy for approval from your senior leader.	High
X			X		Complete an important activity.	Schedule your superusers to support end users in appropriate training classes. Consult with your trainer for questions.	High
X					Complete an important activity.	Determine and schedule staffing needs for cutover, appointment conversion, case conversion, and registration conversion.	Medium
X					Complete an important activity.	Finalize department-specific PTO approach for go-lives, ensuring project needs are prioritized. Communicate expectations with your staff.	Medium

(Continued)

Table 5.4 (Continued) Operational Readiness Checklist

Manager	Providers	Staff	Superusers	SMEs, Op Readiness Lead	Action Required	The following deliverables/tasks should be complete by the months indicated below:	Level of Effort
X					Complete an important activity.	Understand overall ambulatory abstraction strategy and begin to identify how your department will execute. (More readiness items will be added as the overall strategy is defined to ensure your department is prepared.)	Medium
	X			X	Complete an important activity.	By May 6, sign off on future state content build created through the specialty validation process.	Medium
X	X				Complete an important activity.	Submit go-live schedule reduction strategy for administrative approval. (For ambulatory/oncology clinics, schedule reduction based on recommendations.)	Medium
X				X	Communicate effectively.	Present new EHR content/updates as a standing agenda item in your monthly staff meetings (at a minimum) using monthly talking points and roadshow slides for April.	Low

(Continued)

Table 5.4 (Continued)   Operational Readiness Checklist

Manager	Providers	Staff	Superusers	SMEs, Op Readiness Lead	Action Required	The following deliverables/tasks should be complete by the months indicated below:	Level of Effort
End of June							
						June deliverables include key performance indicator (KPI) sign-off, which ensures your departmental metrics are appropriately defined and assigned, as well as the review of training curricula. It is essential that your representative SMEs be involved in the training curriculum review to ensure accurate workflows, relevant exercises, and focused training that will meet end-user expectations.	
				X	Complete a key operational milestone.	Sign off on all your KPIs and radar dashboards for your area.	Medium
X	X		X	X	Complete an important activity.	Participate in end-user application testing. Test key application workflows with the analysts.	Medium
	X			X	Complete an important activity.	Review training curriculum development in preparation for training environment creation. Include a review of patient scenarios and exercises.	High
X				X	Communicate effectively.	Present new EHR content/ updates as a standing agenda item in your monthly staff meetings (at a minimum) using monthly talking points and roadshow slides for May.	Low

Table 5.5   Look Ahead for July 2016 through December 2016

Month	Deliverable
July	• 120-day go-live readiness report out • Revenue cycle testing
August	• 90-day go-live readiness report out • Sign off on charging workflows • Staff registered for training • Hardware deployment
September	• 60-day go-live readiness report out • Superuser training
October	• 30-day go-live readiness report out • Cutover dry run 1 • Legacy data conversion • End-user training • Personalization labs • Hardware testing
November	• Cutover dry run 2 • Cutover • Participate in system demos for your area • End-user training • Competency exam completion • Log-in labs
November- Go-live	• Go-live!

Level of Effort:

■ High: Time consuming and/or complex
■ Medium: Moderate time commitment to complete and/or moderately complex
■ Low: Limited time commitment and/or relatively straightforward to complete

To supplement this short-term task list, the operational readiness checklist should be accompanied by a look ahead leading up to go-live. That long-term view will help provide staff and leaders perspective about where they are headed along the EHR implementation track. Table 5.5 provides a sample look ahead based on the previous checklist. Keep in mind that your checklist should be updated and distributed on a regular basis using no more than 3-month task assignments and a long-term look ahead.

Example Communication 5.3: Operational Readiness Checklist

 Title: Operational Readiness Checklist
Mode of Communication: Email
Target Audience: All Staff
Sent from: Project Team

Operational Readiness Checklist

When the organization began its journey nearly a year ago, it was acknowledged that the new EHR must be more than a "technology" project. Instead it must be owned and embraced by each of us.

The Project Team will require preparation and participation at local levels across the organization. Everyone shares in the responsibility to help ensure success and at this stage, a new tool is being implemented to help departments and areas take action.

To assist with preparations throughout the enterprise, Operational Readiness Checklists are being implemented.

- These checklists have been designed to help ensure everyone is doing the right things at the right times, so we will be well prepared for Go-Live starting later this year.
- The checklist is broken down into activities that must be completed by the end of each month.
- The checklist provides a three-month list of tasks that must be completed, as well as a high-level look ahead to the milestones leading up to the Go-Live date.

To help everyone stay up-to-date on the Operational Readiness Checklists, we have created a special page on the intranet.

In order to ensure accountability for the execution of the checklist items, you will need to implement a status update process. Table 5.6 provides a framework for status updates. The operational areas listed should reflect the operational readiness structure outlined in Figure 5.2. All status updates should be reported to your operational readiness leader on at least a monthly basis.

Example 5.4 includes a sample communication from senior leadership to all staff. The message emphasizes the importance of using the operational readiness checklist to ensure key deliverables that will require significant lead time to complete, such as the development of superuser schedules. Follow-up communications should be sent on a regular basis to highlight upcoming tasks and provide additional details and resources to guide operational leaders (Example 5.5).

Table 5.6   Operational Readiness Status

Operational Area	Readiness Status		
	April	**May**	**June**
Clinical Lab	**Yellow**	**Green**	**Green**
Inpatient Nursing	**Green**	**Green**	**Green**
Pharmacy	**Yellow**	**Red**	**Yellow**
Emergency Department	**Yellow**	**Yellow**	**Yellow**
Hospital Billing	**Red**	**Yellow**	**Green**
Patient Access/Scheduling	**Green**	**Yellow**	**Yellow**

Status Definitions		
Color	Definition	Action Required
Green	No significant issues or concerns and no management action needed. Staff are engaged in all commitments, including SME meetings, training, superuser roles, etc.	None.
Yellow	Issues require attention. Staff are inadequately involved in commitments and managers are actively shifting the focus back to priorities.	Define action plan to return to green status within 15–30 days.
Red	Major barriers are preventing engagement and challenges require immediate intervention from leadership.	Escalate to senior leadership with recommendations for resolution.

Example Communication 5.4: EHR Implementation Update

Title: EHR Implementation Update for Leaders
Mode of Communication: Email
Target Audience: Managers and above
Sent from: CMIO, COO, CNO, CFO
Leaders,

Roadshow slides for May are attached and contain need-to-know information for your checklist completion. Please be sure to do the following:

- Submit completed April checklist to your designated VP/Administrator and readiness workgroup representatives.
- Complete your Operational Readiness Checklist tasks for May.
- Review the below topics and associated actions, and continue to cascade information to your teams.
- Reach out to us, your VP/Administrator, or the appropriate Project Team contact if you have questions.

Additionally, please remember that the estimated timeframes for project milestones are subject to some degree of change. It is frequently necessary to shift a planned activity forward or backward within a given timeframe as issues are discovered or resolved. The most important considerations are that we do things the right way the first time so that we meet our planned Go-Live dates. We will continue to inform you of any changes.

Topic	Description/Talking Points	Call to Action
Operational Readiness Checklists	■ Operational Readiness Checklists for April–June were previously emailed to leaders and are attached with this message (also find them here). Important reminder: – Checklists will be sent quarterly, so you can look and plan ahead. – Checklist tasks should be accomplished and reported monthly. ■ Next quarter checklists (July–Sept) will be distributed in June.	1. Submit April update to your designated VP/administrator and readiness workgroup representatives. 2. Work on May checklist items.
Specialty Provider Training	■ SPTs have been identified to assist with specialty curricula and classroom training for their peers. They will be the first to receive training. ■ Kickoff retreats will provide important introductory information, and SPTs are receiving details about registering.	1. For SPTs, register for a kickoff. 2. Support SPTs during their scheduled activities.
S.U.P.E.R. Program and Superuser Engagement	■ Introducing our new S.U.P.E.R. Program for superusers to remain engaged and receive education leading up to training in September (S.U.P.E.R. = Superuser Preparation, Engagement and Recognition). ■ S.U.P.E.R. Program will include pre-training activities such as E-learnings, Genius Bar events, EHR Playground activities, Workflow Walkthroughs, and more. Superusers will receive an opportunity for rewards/recognition based on participation and increasing levels of knowledge.	1. Encourage superuser involvement in all pre-training activities. 2. Support time commitments needed for superusers. (The more experience superusers gain, the better prepared they will be to support your staff during Training and Go-Lives.)
End-User Training	■ Timeline for end-user training registration has been pushed to early summer.	1. No action is needed from you at this time. Thank you for your patience.

Example Communication 5.5: Guide to Go-Live Content Outline

Title: Guide to Go-Live
Mode of Communication: Email/ Information Packet
Target Audience: All Staff
Sent from: Project Team

**Guide to Go-Live Outline – Provide to All
Staff Within One Month of Go-Live**

- Executive Introduction
  - Since this is intended to be a comprehensive Go-Live document, it is a great opportunity to allow your CEO, CMO, or other executive leadership to introduce Go-Live with a brief note and word of thanks to everyone involved in the project.
- About the Guide to Go-Live
  - Explain what the guide is intended to do – provide important reminders, information, data, logistics, resources, and other information that will help make the Go-Live process easier.
- What to Expect at Go-Live
  - Remind all staff about the importance of operational accountability, appropriate escalation of issues, and the learning curve and continued support that is expected during Go-Live.
  - Offer reassurance that issues are a normal part of the growth and change process.
- Hot Topics for Physicians and Providers
  - Reserve a section for any critical or late-breaking changes or updates that are *specific to physicians*, their workflows, patient care, patient safety, regulatory compliance, or other strategic priorities.
- Go-Live Tips and Support for Physicians and Providers
  - Provide important reminders *for physicians* about topics such as online resources, additional training or support labs or webinars, mobile device access, etc.
- Hot Topics for Nurses and Clinical Staff
  - Reserve a section for any critical or late-breaking changes or updates that are *specific to nurses and clinical staff,* their workflows, patient care, patient safety, regulatory compliance, or other strategic priorities.
- Go-Live Tips and Support for Nurses and Clinical Staff
- Provide important reminders *for nurses and clinical staff* about topics such as online resources, additional training or support labs or webinars, mobile device access, etc.
- Finding Clinical Data Post Go-Live
  - After Go-Live, your organization will likely have converted data from a number of disparate systems into a single EHR. Therefore,

it can be helpful to provide a crosswalk or roadmap for finding specific types of information that users might be accustomed to referencing elsewhere.

- This could include historical results, patient notes, images, and any other information that was converted (or not converted) directly into the new system for a specific period of time.

■ Cutover Timeline

- Provide a high-level overview of the timeline and activities associated with cutover.

■ Downtime Resources

- Remind users where to find current resources they will need for the planned downtime – as well as unplanned downtime, in case it were to occur.

■ FAQs for Common Go-Live Issues

- Common questions you might answer in advance for users include:
  • What should I do if I cannot log in?
  • Where will different types of documents print now?
  • What should I do if something doesn't print where I expected?
  • How can I find a report I need?
  • What should I do if I can't find historical data for a patient?
  • What is the new process for scanning documents into the system?

■ Go-Live Support Roles

- Outline the roles of all support staff who will be part of Go-Live, including superusers and supplemental at-the-elbow support, command center, help desk, training and technical support teams, leaders who will be rounding, etc.

■ Getting Help with Go-Live Issues

- Outline the process for users reporting issues with the new EHR system:
  • Refer to tip sheets and online resources for help.
  • Get help from a superuser or at-the-elbow support.
  • Contact the help desk or command center directly.

■ When to Expect Go-Live Updates

- Provide an outline of daily meetings and updates to ensure leaders and users understand how and when they should expect to receive information during Go-Live.

■ Reminders About Issue Prioritization and Resolution Process

- Reinforce the concept of issue prioritization and set the expectation that critical issues or those impacting large numbers of users will be addressed before other system changes.
- Make sure users have a basic understanding of how the resolution process works – from the time they report an issue to how it is assigned and worked and how the loop will be closed once the issue has been resolved.

■ Appendices
– To shorten content sections within the guide to Go-Live, create appendices to reference supporting documentation from the previous topics or provide other miscellaneous updates.

Key Considerations and Lessons Learned

■ Develop key messaging points and a calendar of when they should be communicated prior to creating individual communications, so you can ensure that messages are consistently aligned using all communications tools. This is especially important as you approach go-live, when time and resources will be taxed.
■ Share information as early as possible, especially if it impacts clinical scheduling, which can occur weeks or months in advance. Key messages you should consider that will impact audiences and scheduling include:
– Scheduling and backfilling plans for superusers, specialty provider trainers (SPTs), and end users involved in training, support, application testing, and other readiness activities.
– Changes to earned time off policies, such as extensions to carryover allowances – since many staff will not have the opportunity to use time off during this period.
– Reductions to patient schedules planned during go-live to allow for stabilization during the transitional period (typically 1–2 weeks).
– Manual conversion and abstraction activities, which are often conducted over a weekend when business offices are typically closed.

Individual Readiness

Organizational and departmental readiness ultimately comes down to individual preparedness. Highlighting this fact should become a critical component of your communication and change leadership strategy. Your EHR implementation will create workflow changes that directly impact individuals on the frontline of patient care. A strong communication plan must include tools, resources, and support documents to help staff through that transitional phase and clarify what the real impacts of the new EHR system will mean to them.

Audience

Readiness describes the ability of an individual to perform their work in the new EHR with a level of proficiency that enables workflows and processes to flow steadily. While your staff will not be optimally efficient or effective at go-live, the goal should be to accelerate the learning curve that will lead to improved efficiency and effectiveness over the long term. Part of accelerating that learning curve will involve targeted communications to specific end-user groups. Those communications should help set expectations and offer activities that will help prepare them for the successful adoption of your new EHR system.

Key Objectives and Message Points

The following are key considerations for assessing the readiness activities of staff and end users by role:

Frontline Staff:
- Understand and can demonstrate new EHR workflows
- Have necessary tools required to perform the job, including hardware and devices
- Know what support tools and resources are available if issues arise

Managers and Supervisors:
- Understand new EHR workflows and the impact on staff roles and responsibilities
- Ensure necessary tools are available for staff to perform the job and serve as an escalation point to address any gaps or needs
- Know what support tools and resources are available if issues arise

Senior Leaders:
- Are equipped to provide support and guidance through the EHR implementation via resource allocation, decision making, and removal of barriers
- Understand the importance of completing key tasks on time and help prioritize strategic work efforts and resources to achieve them
- Establish and support a sense of urgency to ensure managerial and frontline staff are appropriately engaged and prepared
- Hold staff accountable for departmental and individual readiness
- Monitor key performance indicators to evaluate progress

Physicians:

- Understand and can demonstrate new EHR workflows
- Understand where to find legacy information and data that will not be converted to the new EHR
- Have the necessary tools required to perform the job, including hardware and devices
- Know what support tools and resources are available if issues arise
- Complete appropriate customization and personalization options within the new EHR to optimize documentation and workflow efficiency

Communications Tools

The following communications tools will be useful to reach and prepare end users and providers:

- Training classes and online learning
  - Classroom training will likely be the primary method used to educate providers and users about your new EHR system. During the training phase, you can expect to receive feedback (and some resistance) from staff as the changes they will experience become real to them. During training, staff should focus on the individual impacts the new EHR will have on their role and responsibilities, and they should begin building a sense of confidence in their ability to adapt to a new way of working.
- Practice environment
  - A practice environment provides a safe learning space for staff to develop familiarity and proficiency using your new EHR system. This is an essential tool to facilitate individual confidence in the new EHR prior to go-live, since a few hours (or days) of classroom training will not be sufficient to do so.
- Intranet and online
  - Your intranet site should be used to help share and promote the resources and reference tools provided during end-user training. If possible, embed short videos and infographics that highlight important topics and workflow changes.
- Email updates
  - Email updates are typically one of the most utilized and accessible means to reach staff and providers with important and timely messages.

- Keep in mind that while email communications can be quick and easy, overuse of them can create communications fatigue and lead to people "turning off" your message completely.
■ Departmental meetings
  - EHR Project Team leaders should attend regular department meetings across the enterprise (e.g., staff meetings, nurse manager meetings, medical committee meetings) to discuss key milestones, workflow changes, and other topics that impact specific areas.
  - Keep in mind that your new EHR will represent broad change that will need to be translated to specific areas and ultimately individual end users in meaningful terms. It will be important and necessary to have discussions at the local level across your enterprise to understand any concerns or issues and share those details of your EHR launch.
■ Employee forums
  - You should facilitate both broad- and small-scale employee forums to solicit feedback on your overall approach to communications and change. You will need to understand how staff are receiving content, whether they feel appropriately informed, and whether you need to modify your approach.
  - Broad sessions will enable you to gather feedback more quickly and are best suited for groups that can be difficult to coordinate due to clinical responsibilities or other factors (e.g., perioperative staff).
  - Small forums provide greater opportunity for personal dialogue and detailed assessment around individual preparedness and comfort with the new EHR system. Utilizing multiple approaches will give you a holistic view of how well your communication strategy is working and where there are gaps that need to be addressed (Example 5.6).

Example Communication 5.6: Getting Personal About Go-live

Title: Getting Personal About Go-Live
Mode of Communication: Email
Target Audience: All Staff
Sent from: Project Team

Getting Personal About Go-Live

Go-Live has been compared to changing the tires on a car while it is still moving, because healthcare never stops – hospitals are 24/7 operations, and even in medical practices with office hours it's impossible to stop seeing patients long enough to focus exclusively on Go-Live.

We are now less than 90 days from our Go-Live, and based on hundreds of Go-Lives that have come before us, we know there will be lots of ups and downs. Here's what you should expect and what will help make things easier.

Lots of Preparation

During the next three months, the following preparations for Go-Live will be completed:

- Data conversion and abstraction
- Superuser and end-user training
- Self-study and practice in the system
- Hardware deployment
- Dry runs and rehearsals
- Go-Live Readiness Assessments

When Go-Live arrives, everything will seem even more hectic as you care for patients while adjusting to using the new system. To help keep track of what's going on, bookmark and reference this new key dates page on the website.

It has been said that it takes a village to raise a child, and the new EHR is no different. Our project and preparations for Go-Live rest on the broad shoulders of those leaders who have made tremendous contributions and who will continue to do so in the coming months. A special word of thanks is in order for all Guiding Team members

Lots of Stress

Even after going through detailed training and practicing in the Playground (a virtual practice system) leading up to Go-Live, you probably won't feel completely comfortable that you know and understand everything on day one – and that's okay.

- The more you practice in the system prior to Go-Live, the easier the transition will be.
- Biweekly updates leading up to Go-Live will help make sure you understand some of the most frequent issues and should help reduce the stress of the unknown.

Lots of Learning

The learning process leading up to Go-Live will be intense, but it doesn't end there.

- Some issues identified after Go-Live will require system or workflow changes.

- You will need to continue learning as you go.
- The Project Team will be supporting you every step of the way with learning materials and tip sheets.

Lots of Uncertainty

During the time leading up to Go-Live, some people will wonder if we are ready. Rest assured the implementation of the new EHR has been prepared for more extensively than any other system change in the organization's history.

- There are milestones and readiness tools in place to help assess and ensure our readiness.
- You will begin to feel more prepared as you attend classroom training and practice in the system.
- At Go-Live, you and your peers will be supported by an extensive network including superusers, specialty provider trainers, the solution center, Project Team, Training Team, command center, and more.

Lots of Excitement

A wide range of emotions and experiences will come and go during this time, but one thing is certain – Go-Lives are invariably accompanied by lots of excitement and enthusiasm.

- A system-wide transformation of this magnitude is the type of change that many people will only experience once in a lifetime.
- Let's get excited and work together to make sure we are ready to go.
- Others have done this successfully, and so will we!

System Demos and Simulations

System demos and simulations offer another pre go-live activity to facilitate individual and departmental readiness. Because the future state can be vague and feel abstract to staff, system demos are a highly effective way to make things more real. During these sessions, the Project Team will provide an overview of key workflows and processes that demonstrate how work will be done in the new EHR environment. When done effectively, demos and simulations show the story of a patient's journey through the healthcare system, while highlighting new tools, features, and functionalities, and calling out workflow changes in the new EHR system. Table 5.7 outlines some key steps to prepare for system demos.

Table 5.7   Demo/Simulation Checklist

Task	Owner	Duration
Confirm Logistics: • Locations, AV needs, date/time, presenters, SMEs	Lead/ Project manager	1–2 weeks
Finalize demo/simulation workflow selection	Application analysts	3–5 weeks
Update scripts and scenario	Application analysts	3 weeks
Identify operational SMEs to contribute	Application analysts and operational owners	1–2 weeks
Configure demo/simulation in playground system environment	Application analysts	4–6 weeks
WFWT Rehearsals	Application analysts	1 week
WFWT Event Day 1	All	1–5 days

Examples of demos and simulations:

■ Ambulatory office visit
■ Emergency department to operating room
■ Operating room to ICU
■ Radiology workflows
■ Patient portal self-scheduling/online bill pay

Where possible, superusers and subject matter experts should be included in the actual presentation and simulations rather than the EHR Project Team staff. The demos will carry more weight if staff members see their colleagues using the new system and talking through its benefits. Leveraging staff for the demos can also provide an opportunity to highlight the support and other resources that will be available during go-live (Example Communication 5.7).

Example Communication 5.7: System Demos

Title: System Demo Updates
Mode of Communication: Email
Target Audience: All Staff
Sent from: Project Team

The **system demos** provided the community with a first look into the newly designed system. Over 3 days, close to 500 staff members attended sessions related to both clinical workflows as well as access and revenue cycle workflows.

Three of the demos are showcased below.

The Outpatient Journey

This integrated demonstration features a patient's Outpatient Visit, starting with their Primary Care doctor and ending with scheduling a surgery for thyroid removal. **WATCH VIDEO** (01:26)

If you don't wish to watch the entire Outpatient Journey, advance to the following times to see various sections of the integrated demonstration.

- 8:34 to see a patient schedule an appointment through the patient portal
- 12:30 to see a patient checked in
- 15:45 to see a patient with a nurse being prepped to see the doctor
- 10:40 to see a patient visit with the Primary Care Physician
- 31:30 to see a Primary Care Physician order a referral for general surgery
- 33:10 to see a patient visit with the surgeon
- 44:05 to see Referral Work Queues
- 47:24 to see a patient visit with a cardiologist
- 53:20 Q&A session

The Future Patient Portal

This demonstration shows the robust future patient portal and its features, including reviewing lab results, patient educational materials, and the ability to schedule doctors' appointments, among many others. **WATCH VIDEO** (00:30)

Access and Revenue Cycle: The Future in Referral Processing

This demonstration shows how referrals will be processed by staff members using the Referral Work Queue feature and highlights the importance of ensuring referrals are worked in the queue on a regular basis. **WATCH VIDEO** (00:31)

Go-Live Logistics

Operational readiness also includes go-live logistics preparation. Table 5.8 is an example of a go-live logistics checklist for operational leaders.

Table 5.8 Go-Live Logistics Checklist

Department/ Division:			
Person Completing Form:			
Topic	*Task*	*Due Date*	*Supporting Details/ Guidance*
Training			
Superusers	Have all superusers been identified for all roles (including providers) at all of your practice locations going live?	30 Sept	Ratios of superusers to end users has been determined by location and shift. Superusers were submitted 4/1 and a subsequent gap analysis was conducted. Please confirm you have adequate internal support for your end users, as this is an operational responsibility.
Superusers	Have all superusers been registered for training courses based on their roles and any cross-training for additional roles they might need to support within the department?	12 Aug	Training catalogue and online course calendar.
Superusers	Have your superusers completed assigned e-learnings?	12 Sept	Training catalogue and online course calendar.
Superusers	Have your superusers completed training?	3 Oct	Training catalogue and online course calendar.

(*Continued*)

Table 5.8 (Continued) Go-Live Logistics Checklist

Topic	Task	Due Date	Supporting Details/ Guidance
Superusers	Have all of your superusers been scheduled to provide end-user training support? (Superusers are taken out of the clinical schedule for go-live; they do not take clinical or operational assignments during their superuser shift.)	30 Sept	Training catalogue and online course calendar.
End Users	Have all end users been registered for training and completed or scheduled e-learning prerequisites prior to the start of training?	16 Sept	Make sure people are appropriately enrolled in the right courses to have correct security/access per their role/ responsibilities.
Specialty Provider Trainer (SPT)	Have all SPTs attended training and allocated time for self-study?	9 Sept	SPTs are responsible for training their peers through specialty-specific workflows in the new system. This will optimize in-class training and decrease in-class time for provider end users by 50% and promote more effective use of and proficiency with specialty-specific tools.
Schegistration	Have front-end staff completed pre-EHR insurance education classes?	23 Sept	Insurance 101/102 training sessions for staff working within new Schegistration model.
Clinical Operations			
Hardware	Have you confirmed the correct hardware is deployed in your areas and designated provider workstations?	14 Oct	Hardware deployments will finalize in early September. Please ensure the IT staff have access to your practices in order to install/replace equipment.

(Continued)

Table 5.8 (Continued)   Go-Live Logistics Checklist

Topic	Task	Due Date	Supporting Details/ Guidance
Hardware	Has the Project Team scheduled their hardware testing site visits with your practices?	1 Oct	During hardware testing, the Project Team tests workflows on each device that is used during go-live. The team verifies that all hardware is integrating correctly with the new EHR, including label printers, paper printers, barcode scanners, document scanners and printers, and other relevant devices.
Hardware	Have you confirmed all printers have green stickers adhered? Also, have you ensured that all printers in clinical areas have a sticker (red or green)?	1 Oct	Once hardware testing is complete, technicians will place a green sticker on the printer to verify it passed testing. Please communicate to staff regarding what the green stickers mean and not to remove them.
Appointment Conversion	Beginning November 1, has staff been resourced to begin placing appointments manually into the new EHR?	14 Oct	Manually convert appointments from legacy to the new system and manually update missing registration information from converted accounts to complete registration.

- ■ Superusers/End Users/Training
  - – Training enrollment
  - – Course attendance and completion
  - – System practice and competency verification
- ■ Staffing/Backfill
  - – During training
  - – During go-live through 4–5 weeks post go-live
- ■ Patient Schedule
  - – Frontloading schedules (4–5 months pre go-live)
  - – Reducing schedules (1–3 weeks post go-live)
- ■ Hardware/Devices
  - – Installed and tested

- Conversions
  - Appointment and case conversions from legacy to new EHR (typically 3–4 weeks pre go-live)
  - Data conversion and abstraction

Physicians will want to know details specific to the transition of legacy systems, including what data and information to expect in the new system and where to find it. There is a good chance that not all data and documents will be converted, so you will need to provide instructions on where to get the needed information. Example 5.8 provides a sample of how clinical data conversion can be communicated.

Example Communication 5.8: Data Conversion, Abstraction, and Cutover

Title: Data Conversion, Abstraction, & Cutover
Mode of Communication: Email
Target Audience: All Staff
Sent from: Project Team

What are data conversion, abstraction, and cutover, and why are they important?

- Most data will be moved from current systems using automated methods of data conversion that are built and managed by the Project Team.
- Some additional data will need be manually converted or abstracted.
- All converted data will be made "live" when cutover is finalized at Go-Live.
- Generally, you can expect the following systems and information to be part of the transition:
  - Population of patients across hospital and outpatient practices
  - Scheduling, registration, and billing information
  - Outpatient EHR, including problems, medications, allergies, vaccinations and clinical notes
  - Hospital EHR, including encounters and clinical results, allergies, and vaccinations
  - Transplant system information

Final Preparation and Motivation

Your EHR go-live will mark a significant milestone for your organization. The months, weeks, and days leading up to go-live will be full of anxiety, concern, and uneasiness. Senior leadership support will be a prerequisite for success. As such, it is important to have senior leaders clearly visible and in front of the change – driving messages that reinforce individual and operational readiness (Example Communication 5.9).

Example Communication 5.9: Message from the CEO

Title: Message from the CEO
Mode of Communication: Email
Target Audience: All Staff
Sent from: CEO

To All Employees

We are just a few days away from our Go-Live. Innovation is at the heart of the organization's vision and values, and this transformation to this new EHR will better prepare us to shape and innovate the future of exceptional healthcare.

While most of you won't actually use the system until Monday, many practices will be experiencing the new EHR over the weekend at an optimal, off-peak time when patient volumes are lower. Whether you are working this weekend or will begin your life in the new EHR next week, I'm appreciative of the incredible hours all of you have put into getting us ready for this transformation.

The experience during Go-Live has been compared to changing the tires on a car while it's still moving. That's because healthcare never stops, and neither have the teams dedicated to this monumental project. To the teams from IT, the EHR Project, Clinical Operations, Revenue Cycle, and many others working behind the scenes, thank you for your commitment to driving this forward. Let's be proud of all that you have accomplished:

- More than 1000 of you served as subject matter experts in 350+ Validation sessions.
- About 1800 superusers and specialty providers have been trained.
- More than 5000 new devices have been deployed within 90 days.
- We completed the build, including testing and transition of the entire software platform to a virtualized environment.
- Plans are in place to formally retire more than 40 legacy applications.

And these numbers just scratch the surface.

For you, this Go-Live will be a memorable experience because of the massive accomplishments to date, and how you have prepared for it. There will be some rough patches, for sure, but we'll get through them because of the dedication and determination I consistently see in all of you. And when we hit those patches, we must remind ourselves of why we are doing all of this in the first place – it's for our patients and their families – to provide them with a seamless experience they can always count on.

Thank you for everything you are doing for all of us, have a great Thanksgiving and good luck as we count down to a very important milestone!

Metrics Strategy

Continuous improvement is mandatory in a high-stakes project such as EHR deployment. You should constantly be assessing what is working, and what could be changed to achieve better outcomes. This section will review some of the mechanisms you can use to solicit feedback, analyze your communications vehicles, and improve your communications strategy during the course of the project.

Before launching your communications plan, you must understand who should be engaged during each phase. While virtually everyone in the organization should be aware of high-level information, you should establish early and often that specific segments of your enterprise will not be engaged directly. Set expectations around your strategy with leadership, so there isn't the expectation of 100 percent participation or readership for all communications.

To begin the process, it is important to set a baseline for your organization's typical read rate so you can measure your success based on what is normal for your culture. Without a baseline, you may find yourself shooting in the dark to make a judgment on the impact of your communications.

Electronic communications metrics are relatively new to the communications field but have gained popularity during the past 10-15 years with the rise of electronic tracking tools. Internal communications teams are also finding it necessary to measure engagement more actively now to help cut through the noise that is constantly competing for their audiences' attention. In today's world of communications, metrics are more than a "nice-to-have." They are an essential part of ensuring your organization is informed and ready. Metrics will also be a useful component to share with C-level and operational leadership teams, especially when organizational stress starts to increase or when staff begin to complain that they "don't know anything."

Surveys

Surveys are a quick and easy way to assess the responsiveness and engagement of staff. We have already covered the importance of baseline surveys to inform your communications strategy, but there will also be numerous opportunities during your EHR implementation project to use targeted surveys on a smaller scale. For example, you may want to garner feedback from the following groups of users.

Survey SMEs immediately after they attend validation to improve the next session's experience:

■ What went well with the sessions?
■ How can we improve the next sessions?
■ What is unclear?
■ What questions or concerns do you have after attending?

Survey superusers before and after training:

■ What additional support do you need?
■ Is the training sufficient?
■ What other resources would help you gain proficiency?
■ What are the needs of your department?

Survey provider/specialty providers before and after training:

■ What additional support do you need?
■ Is the training sufficient?
■ What other resources would help you gain proficiency?
■ What are the needs of your department?

Survey SMEs for post-stabilization enhancement and optimization

■ Post go-live, there will be a period of adjustment to the new system and its workflows. However, a survey can be incorporated into the planning for the next phases of system enhancement and growth based on employee suggestions and ideas for the future.

Email Readership Tracking System

Email metrics track the reach and open rate for communications. Usually, this requires a paid subscription negotiated annually, individual user accounts, and Outlook plugins for each user. Depending on your budget, you may want to evaluate multiple email measurement tools to determine which service offers the best value, while also meeting the requirement of maintaining control of enterprise email lists without the need to host and maintain them using an outside server.

The following charts represent snapshots of various types of email communications during different time periods of the project (Figures 5.3 through 5.6).

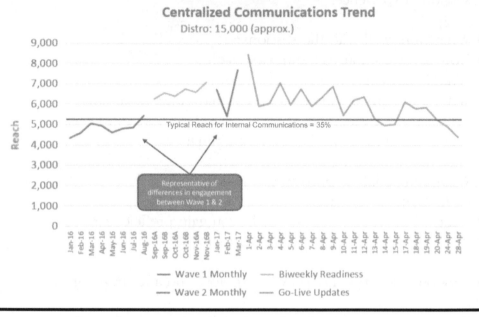

Figure 5.3   Email newsletter metrics throughout the life of a project.

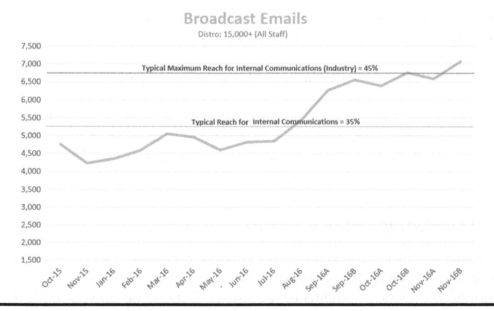

Figure 5.4   Tracking all-employee executive memos.

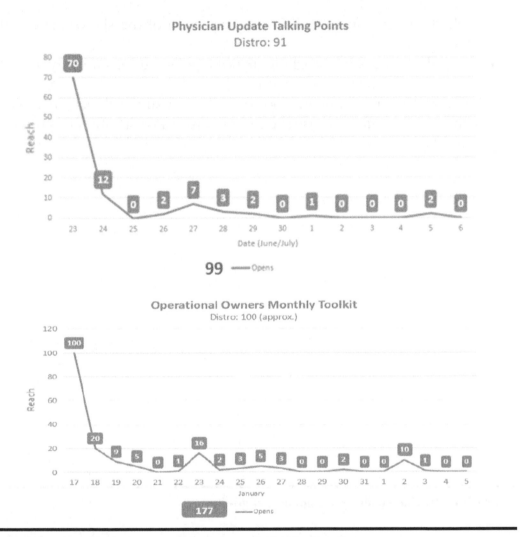

Figure 5.5 Tracking open rates for targeted distribution lists.

Web Readership Tracking System

Tracking the hits on your project intranet site will be helpful when assessing what information is most interesting and impactful to your end users. Google Analytics offers free tools that can be used to measure activities on your intranet. If you have a Google account and Gmail address, it is quite simple to attach your intranet site to the analytics platform for easy tracking.
   Some tips for usage:

■ The "Content Drilldown" menu option in the left navigation under "Behavior" is a particularly useful section for reviewing detailed metrics for individual sections and pages. Traffic can be easily tracked within a specific directory or section of the site or for specific pages.

◼ Check date ranges in Google Analytics regularly to ensure they are set to report the desired time period.

◼ Behavior Flow reporting in Google Analytics will not directly correlate with overall traffic, because the report is based on a subset of visitors to a site (Figure 5.7).

Figure 5.6 Tracking daily email updates at go-live.

Measurement Themes

Depending on the maturity of your feedback mechanisms, you may find those gained through electronic tracking the most useful. Some common themes to look out for include:

◼ Insight into what days and times during the week employees tend to open and read emails and visit the web. You can use this to redirect your most important messages during those timeframes.

◼ Confirmation that segmented electronic communications targeting different audiences are more effective than broad catch-all newsletters/ bulletins that target all users. For example, in a use case from a physician communications and engagement campaign (also discussed in

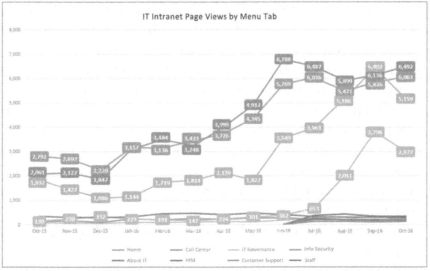

Figure 5.7   Using site analytics.

Chapter 3), rates were anywhere from 60 percent to 97 percent, compared to 35–45 percent among all employees. This shows that due to
the nature of more targeted, relevant content, the physician population
read their emails on a more regular basis.

■ Blast or targeted emails from executives are more likely to get a higher
readership rate based on the credibility and respect that comes with
specific leaders and their ability to influence and engage employees.
Emails from generic inboxes can often be ignored or deleted. For newsletters or other branded project communications, it can be helpful to
use the subject line to let employees know that there is an important

message from a high-level leader so they are more likely to open the email.

■ When readership is low on the intranet, you have several options. You can dig deeper to find which particular articles, documents, or videos get the most clicks and then replicate content and models that mirror the most popular content. If your intranet metrics are consistently low, this may simply be a product of your culture and represent the need to use other channels more proficiently, while replicating the content on the web in other ways.

■ Metrics should also be used for overall insight into the health of end-user engagement. For example, in the early stages, before the reality of the implementation sets in, it is natural to see low readership rates. However, as your call to action for involvement, training, and operational readiness increases through your messaging, so should your readership. Consistently low rates halfway through the project and beyond can be a red flag and may require special intervention.

■ Low readership rates can be used to call for more leadership involvement/intervention. For example, if your communications strategy relies heavily on electronic communication due to your early survey results indicating email as the primary preference for employees, but your email open rate is low, you have an argument to bring to leaders about their support and reinforcement of the information. You can use this data to create an accountability agreement for leaders to require their employees to read emails about the project.

■ Most activity occurs within two business days of sending (Table 5.9):
  – May Update
    • ~500 opens within 1–2 hours of sending (Business Day 1).
    • ~1000 opens by end of day (Business Day 1).
    • ~1500 opens by noon Monday (Business Day 2).
  – June Update
    • Multiple repeat opens within two business days shows strong engagement by specific leaders.

The Communicator's Challenge

If you are a communications professional, one of your primary challenges will be the inability to please everyone and check all the boxes with your communications. For first-time implementations, it can be overwhelming when understanding what feedback to prioritize. Resources and the size of

Table 5.9 Two-Month Comparison of Targeted Provider Metrics

Provider Communication	Distro	Opens	Reach	Links	Clicks	Attachments (Not Measurable)
May update Sent: Friday, 05/12, just after noon	~2,600	1,834	~70%	Post go-live survey links, email Thrive (post go-live training) registration, tip sheets (5)	94	New post-op progress note type, May enhancement details
June update Sent: Thursday, 06/15, just before noon	~2,700 (added resident contacts)	1,642	~60%	On/off-boarding residents info, questionnaire details, tip sheets (2)	81	June enhancement details

your communications team will, of course, influence your ability to execute and change strategy mid-stream.

Therefore, just as you should set expectations about your readership goals (e.g., to be at or above the baseline of the typical organizational rate), you should also set expectations about who you will take and implement feedback from, as well as the associated turnaround time for major changes.

The following inputs are recommended:

- The highest governance organizing body (i.e., the guiding team)
- Your project leadership, specifically the CIO, CMIO, or Executive Project Director
- Periodic insights from electronic metrics (i.e., a quarterly review and amendment/tweaking of your communications plan)

Piecemeal anecdotal feedback from individual employees or departments must have a mechanism for review, and employee's voices must be acknowledged, but it is impossible to prioritize or implement all feedback. When in doubt, refer to your guiding principles, governance model, and project leadership for guidance.

Chapter 6

Launch

It is difficult to overstate the intensity and importance of your go-live. That time, which bridges Transition and Future stages in the Communications and Change Leadership Model, is when many months (or years) of work will culminate in a single cutover event that will change the course of your organization for decades. The complexity and rapid pace of go-live will require a robust and carefully planned schedule of communications to keep your leaders and staff informed. Basic contingency plans and accompanying communications strategies are also important, in the event cutover is problematic or unplanned downtimes occur. By putting these communications plans in place and remaining flexible and responsive to the issues that will invariably arise, you can rest assured that you will be ready to engage and inform your audiences in virtually any situation (Figure 6.1 and Table 6.1).

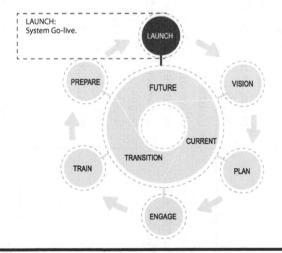

Figure 6.1   Launch.

Table 6.1 In This Section

Activity	Primary Objectives	Key Messages	Communications Tools
6.1 Go-Live: Cutover	• Communicate details needed by staff leading up to and during cutover, when the new EHR system is made live. • Have contingency and crisis communications plans in place, in the event they are needed.	• There are a number of tasks the Project Team will handle during cutover, as well as activities that clinical and operational staff will need to complete.	• Email updates: Details outlining timelines and expectations • Intranet site: Resources and tools for troubleshooting, issue reporting, and system fixes • Decentralized meetings: Led by Project Team to discuss specific risks, issues, and expectations
6.2 Go-Live: Cutover + 1 Week	• Utilize daily updates and other communications to ensure leadership and staff are aware of any widespread issues, as well as the resolutions and resources available to make the first week of go-live easie r.	• Share current updates and resolutions for any widespread issues. • Link to resources, tip sheets, etc., that support issues or user questions. • Provide details for ongoing training opportunities, workshops, etc. • Share success stories from go-live.	• Email updates: Details outlining timelines and expectations • Intranet site: Resources and tools for troubleshooting, issue reporting, and system fixes • Decentralized meetings: Led by Project Team to discuss specific risks, issues, and expectations
6.3 Go-Live: Cutover + 2–4 Weeks (Normalization)	• Adjust communications to meet the needs of users as they begin to normalize with the new EHR system.	• What are the expectations for normalization, and how are we doing? • Continue to share updates, resources, and success stories from go-live as they become more common.	• Email updates: Details outlining timelines and expectations • Intranet site: Resources and tools for troubleshooting, issue reporting, and system fixes • Decentralized meetings: Led by Project Team to discuss specific risks, issues, and expectations

Go-Live: Cutover

Cutover is the brief but critical few hours when current systems will be turned off and the new electronic health record (EHR) system will be made live for use by all staff members across the enterprise.

Audience

Leading up to and during the cutover from your current systems to the new EHR, you should provide several updates to all staff – the first a few weeks in advance, again 1–2 days prior, as well as immediately before and after the cutover is completed (See Example Communication 6.1).

Key Objectives and Message Points

- What changes will occur during cutover?
- What actions must clinical and operational staff take in preparation for and during cutover?

Communications Tools

- Email updates
  - Email updates are typically one of the most utilized and accessible means to reach the enterprise with important and timely messages.
  - Keep in mind that while email communications can be quick and easy, overuse of them can create communications fatigue and lead to people "turning off" your message completely.

Example Communication 6.1: Overview of Cutover Timeline

Title: Overview of Cutover Timeline
Mode of Communication: Email
Target Audience: All Staff
Sent from: Project Team

Overview of Cutover Timeline

- Cutover is the time when current systems will be turned off and the EHR production system will be made live for use by all staff members.

- The following timeline will be used for cutover during the Inpatient Go-Live.
- If this timeline changes based on events during the cutover period, notifications will be sent out informing all users of the changes.

Details for Providers, Nursing, and Clinical Staff – Must Read for Staff Involved in Cutover

You will be supported by Cutover Teams in two command centers who will be actively coordinating key events and resolving any issues throughout the cutover period.

TO DO: Friday, March 31, 7 am to Saturday, April 1, 12 am

- In legacy EHR, clean up orders.
- In legacy EHR, co-sign orders and notes.
- In new EHR, do not attempt to place orders or document notes.

TO DO: Friday, March 31, 8 pm to Saturday, April 1, 12 am

- 10 pm – Blood bank type and screen results will no longer pass into legacy EHR.
- 11:30 pm
  - Imaging system will be down.
  - Images should be read prior to 11:30 pm. For any image not read by that time AND any new orders, positive results will be called in by a radiologist and negative results will be faxed.
  - During this time, nursing will need to complete paper radiology requisition forms to be sent with patients to any studies.
- 12 am
  - All phlebotomy draws, including nursing collections, must be complete.
  - Users stop entering orders in legacy EHR.
  - New EHR armbands will be delivered by midnight and shall be placed on the patients by nursing staff before 5 am. Legacy EHR arm bands should not be removed until the new EHR is live.

TO DO: Saturday April 1, 12 am to 7 am

- 12 am
  - All paper orders need to go to pharmacy:
    - ADT messages will not be available – Patients new to the unit will need to be keyed in manually into the pharmacy system to withdraw medications.

- Use downtime procedures and/or document on paper for the following:
  - Legacy EHR, which will be in read-only mode:
    - Order entry will not be available.
    - Registration will not be available – except for Emergency Department (ED).
    - Legacy EHR will print out Medication Administration Profile and census lists.
    - Nursing will continue to document flowsheets.
  - New phlebotomy order paper requisitions slated for morning collection will be posted on doors by nursing.
  - Point of care devices.
  - Blood product orders.
- What will still be working:
  - ADT interface to ED documentation system.
  - Imaging viewer.
  - Lab Results icon will be available.
  - Pharmacy medication dispensing machines (in override mode).
  - Lab system for lab results filing into legacy and new EHR.

■ 2 am
  - Lab system will be disconnected from instruments:
    - Due to manual process, turnaround times will be slower.
    - Lab call center will be operational for support.

■ 3:15 am
  - Glucometers should be re-docked by nurses (confirm blank screen and re-dock).

■ 4 am
  - Pre-printed progress notes will not be printed for providers.

■ 5 am
  - New EHR released to end users:
    - Everything will be current in the new EHR except Nursing Checklist items.
    - Nurses complete checklist "After Live Charting Priorities Document."
  - Nurses cut off legacy EHR wrist band after completing checklist above:
    - Point of Care remains on paper until removing the legacy EHR wrist bands.
  - Recovery from planned downtime:
    - Progress notes can be entered by providers in the new EHR and pended until intake and output (I&Os) and vitals are entered by nursing staff (approximately 7 am).

- Pharmacy medication dispensing system will be off override mode as soon as possible:
    ■ Nurses will receive communication to confirm.
■ 7 am
    – I&Os and vitals should be completed/entered in the new EHR by nurses.
    – Pended physician notes can be completed.

Updates to Lab Draw Schedule and Point of Care Testing for Cutover

Friday, March 31: Early Morning Collect Lab Draws During Cutover

■ Early Morning Collect (10 pm–3 am collections) – phlebotomists will start at 8 pm and must be complete by midnight.
■ Blood bank will be down at 10 pm and will need paper requisitions or legacy EHR screenshots to accompanying blood draws that are going to the department.
■ All nursing collections must also be completed and in the lab by midnight.

Saturday, April 1: Morning Collect Lab Draws During Cutover

■ Morning Collect (4 am collections) – phlebotomists' start-time will be postponed until approximately 5 am after the Project Team cutover is completed.
■ In the event of any unexpected delays during cutover, phlebotomists and staff should be prepared to do morning collection on paper using the legacy lab system.
    – For information regarding this potential process, refer to the Clinical Systems Downtime Policy on the Intranet Webpage.

Point of Care Testing

■ Must be documented on paper starting at midnight on Friday, March 31, and continuing into Saturday morning – until notification that the new EHR cutover is completed, the new system is available for staff use, and patients have armbands removed.

Go-Live: Cutover + 1 Week

During the first week of go-live, you should expect a large number (hundreds, or even thousands) of issues to be reported, many of which will be critical in nature. It is important to have a well-structured plan for regular daily communications, as well as the flexibility to react and communicate quickly, when needed.

Audience

Since go-live impacts virtually the entire enterprise (or an entire portion of the enterprise, if you are using a phased or "big bang" approach), there are several key audiences that should receive focused communications during the first week of go-live. They can generally be categorized as follows:

■ Providers and clinical staff
■ Front desk and scheduling staff
■ Back office and billing staff
■ All users (general messaging)

For large projects, it is worth considering whether to further segment your audiences and deliver messages for more specific groups as follows:

■ Providers
■ Interprofessional staff (e.g., nursing, case management, pharmacy, rehab, etc.)
■ Emergency department
■ Ancillary services (lab, radiology, etc.)
■ Perioperative
■ Scheduling
■ Billing
■ All users (general messaging)

 Factor the size and resources of your communications team when determining the approach you will take. Because frequent communications will be needed during go-live, it is better to use a simpler approach that can be consistently executed than a robust strategy that cannot be maintained! Instead of creating separate communications, a single one can be created with sections for specific audiences. This allows for targeted messaging while reducing the time and resources required to execute separate communications.

Key Objectives and Message Points

The most effective go-live updates will contain a variety of content that can be rotated as needed. Generally, you will want to ensure your updates include the following components:

- Current updates and resolutions for any widespread issues
- Links to resources, tip sheets, etc. that support issues or user questions
- Details for ongoing training opportunities, workshops, etc.
- Success stories and go-live photos

Communications Tools

The following tools should be part of a successful go-live communications strategy:

- Email updates
  - You may find during your implementation leading up to go-live that email will be the best way to reach the most people effectively. Keep in mind that the content collection process during a 24/7-pace inpatient go-live will be difficult. You want to maintain a balance of high-level updates that impact all employees and more specific updates by role/department to ensure your work is adding value for everyone.
  - Regular updates should be planned at least once daily within the first week of go-live.
  - Inpatient environments may require weekend and/or evening updates during the first 1–2 weeks of go-live, since they are staffed 24/7.
  - Ambulatory and/or outpatient environments do not generally require weekend updates.
  - Be sure to consider outliers such as urgent care centers or other offices that remain open for extended hours and might need support or communications.
- Intranet and online
  - Intranet and other internal web pages can be used to archive go-live updates and other information, as well as to provide more details about summary issues that are pushed out via daily email updates.

- Online pages are a good way to quickly and efficiently share go-live photos, "quick wins," and success stories that are shared from leadership and staff.
■ Text messages
  - Text messages can be an effective way to provide urgent updates, especially to leaders.
  - Texts can also be paired with email notifications to provide a multimodal approach for communications in the event of emergent needs.
  - This communication method should be used sparingly and only for the highest level issues, to avoid communication fatigue.
■ Meetings and conference calls
  - A robust, carefully planned, and well-executed meeting strategy is one of the most effective ways to communicate issues and get feedback during go-live.
  - Meetings should be scheduled on a regular basis to share information and keep the following groups informed:
    • Executive leadership
    • Operational leadership
    • Service lines by EHR application
    • Superusers
    • Project leadership and project teams
  - Meeting schedules should be coordinated with the timing of other communications to ensure the efficient and effective flow of information throughout the day (see the example meeting schedule in Table 6.2).
■ Blogs
  - Blogs can be used to push information and provide an alternative for direct feedback or two-way communications.
  - Because a timely response is key to interaction, blogs are a resource-intensive strategy and should be carefully evaluated based on available resources to ensure feasibility.
■ Knowledgebase
  - A knowledgebase or similar repository for reference documents and tip sheets is extremely important during go-live, since communications will frequently need to reference those resources during the course of issue resolution.

Table 6.2 Go-Live Meeting Schedule

Daily Timing	Meeting/Communication Tool	Key Participants
6:30–7:30 am	EHR application team huddles Morning shift handoffs	EHR application analyst, managers, superusers
7am–12 pm	Operational department meetings	EHR application analyst, operational leaders, superusers
12–1 pm	Top issues prep meeting	Internal review by EHR managers and operational leaders
1–2 pm	Top issues review	All end users and leaders
4–5 pm	Executive status update	Executive leadership, EHR leadership
6–6:30 pm	Daily email blast	All end users
6:30–7:30 pm	Evening shift handoff	Superusers, operational leaders
Ongoing	Website updates, emergency/ urgent alerts 24/7	All end users

A significant challenge to timely communications during go-live is the creation of new tip sheets and other reference documents. Those resources, which are needed to support the resolution of system issues and problematic workflows, must be created by training and documentation staff and vetted by all parties involved. If needed, communications might need to be distributed without an immediate link to such resources. Under those circumstances, refer to the pending document, but be careful not to turn daily go-live updates into a collection of extended content that should be contained in tip sheets and other references.

■ Practice environment
  – The practice environment should remain open during go-live in case users have questions and want to test functionality.
  – REMINDER: It will be important to remind staff that, after go-live, they should not "practice" in the live EHR system. Any practice activities should be done in the designated practice or playground environment that has been set up for that purpose.

■ Provider personalization and support sessions
  – Personalization and support labs are useful when physicians and providers need hands-on support for common go-live issues.
  – These sessions also help reassure clinicians that continued support is available from specialty provider trainers and other training team members.
■ Surveys
  – Feedback should be collected through formal survey tools, as well as anecdotally through a variety of means such as a central email address promoted in the daily updates, or polls during leadership rounding.
  – TIP: Give leaders survey cards to easily record common feedback that is shared during rounding. These cards can also be used to provide leadership talking points.

Timing

Timing is especially important to consider with go-live updates, since there will be a significant level of activity during this time, and staff will be more distracted than usual. Here are some of the benefits and caveats of providing updates at different times:

Morning
■ Early morning updates (prior to 7 am) can be helpful for providing information to large numbers of inpatient clinical staff before they start their daytime shift.
■ These updates are typically more difficult to execute, based on the availability of information, as well as the leadership and staff needed to compile relevant details and obtain necessary approvals overnight.

Midday
■ Some staff, especially leadership, might take a brief break to check email during lunchtime – making midday a viable alternative for daily updates.
■ These updates are often more feasible than early morning. However, since many issues tend to develop and remain ongoing throughout the daytime, and Project Team members will be actively working on those issues, information or updates can be difficult to compile for a midday communication.

Evening

■ Evening updates are often preferred, as they will accomplish several goals and can be easier to facilitate:
  – Adequate time for the development, collection, and vetting of issues and potential resolutions from project teams throughout the day.
  – Opportunities for leaders and staff to review updates after work stops in the ambulatory environment or when volume often tends to slow in many inpatient environments. Additionally, leaders or staff who don't check email in the evening should find the previous day's update near the top of their inboxes the following morning.
  – Current updates for overnight inpatient staff as they begin their shift. This can be helpful since there is often less direct support available during nighttime hours.
  – Sufficient communications and leadership to prepare and finalize updates.

Real-Time Updates

■ Because issues during go-live are complex and constantly evolving, real-time updates can be difficult or impossible to execute in great detail (Figure 6.2). However, there are times when real-time – or emergent – updates will be needed to address issues that cannot wait for a daily update. Use the following guidelines:
  – Real-time updates during go-live are only advised for significant enterprise-wide issues, such as an unplanned downtime, the complete outage of a critical service or system, etc.
  – In the event an update is needed in real time for a critical issue, it should be accomplished through coordination with project leadership and by leveraging existing communications channels and processes (i.e., help desk or service center), if possible.

Key Considerations and Lessons Learned

Go-live email updates can be managed and executed through a third-party service if budget and other constraints allow. These services typically offer benefits including easier editing, additional formatting options, greater consistency of format, and built-in tracking metrics.

■ CAUTION: Many third-party services require uploading your email lists to an external server in order to send messages. Though there

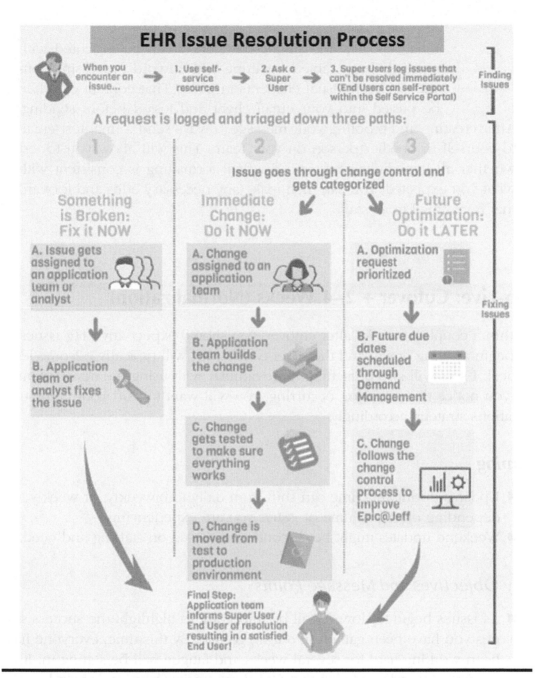

Figure 6.2 Issue resolution process.

should not be protected health information (PHI) or other confidential details included in the go-live updates, the idea of uploading email addresses for an entire organization might present security concerns. Be sure to ask vendors if this is a potential concern for your organization.

Email updates and simple newsletters can be executed with relatively basic table formatting within word processing software to keep visual elements in place. That content can then be pasted into your email client and tested before sending. After creating and proofing your message, always send a final test email to yourself or another person on your team. This will allow you to test whether all hyperlinks work and the final formatting is consistent with what you expected. You can then make any necessary edits and forward that final email to all staff.

Go-Live: Cutover + 2–4 Weeks (Normalization)

Within a couple of weeks after cutover, you should expect any EHR issues to begin slowing down, and the severity of issues will typically become less critical. Users will also be getting more familiar with using the new system. As you notice that transition occurring, you will want to shift your communications strategy accordingly.

Timing

- Updates during this time can shift from daily to biweekly, or weekly depending on the volume of issues you are experiencing.
- Weekend updates might be discontinued, based on staffing and need.

Key Objectives and Message Points

- As issues begin to slow, it will be important to highlight the success stories you have been gathering during go-live. By this time, everyone has been working hard for several weeks and fatigue will be setting in. It is important to acknowledge that and share positive stories to help keep morale high.

Chapter 7

Life After Go-Live

Following go-live, your organization will likely need to take a "breather" to recover from the rigorous schedule that comes with cutover, issue resolution, and go-live support. From a change management perspective, this break will also allow staff to adjust to using the new EHR system and workflows in the new current state, before any additional changes are made. Within 1 to 2 months after go-live, you should have an established plan in place to resume regular communications about ongoing system optimization, enhancement, and maintenance. These post go-live activities will help ensure that you are consistently improving the EHR, fixing issues as they are identified, addressing requests from users, applying security patches, and implementing new functionalities (Table 7.1).

Post Go-Live: Break-Fix, Optimizations, and Enhancements

Shortly after go-live, you should expect to enter a period of relative stability using the new EHR system. However, numerous changes will continue to be needed in the form of break-fix for issues that are identified, as well as optimizations and enhancements to improve workflows and EHR functionality.

Audience

Many of the fixes, optimizations, and enhancements that are made to your EHR will be based on requests from physicians and providers, operations or clinical staff in a specific discipline, business office and financial leadership,

Table 7.1   In This Section

Activity	Primary Objectives	Key Messages	Communications Tools
7.1 Post Go-Live: Break-Fix, Optimizations, and Enhancements	• Convey fixes for any issues that are discovered after go-live. • Communicate key changes that are made to streamline system functionality and make workflows more efficient (optimizations), as well as those that will add new functionality (enhancements).	• Go-live was only the beginning of the transformation with our new EHR system. • Leaders and operational staff need to continue providing feedback and should remain engaged to ensure we can improve our EHR system collaboratively.	• Email updates: Specific fixes with broad impacts and key system updates • Intranet articles highlighting key wins, impact of new EHR, and employee experiences • Decentralized meetings: Discuss specific issues/opportunities for ongoing improvements and system enhancements
7.2 Post Go-Live: Scheduled Downtimes and Maintenance	• Ensure staff are aware of planned downtimes and periods of limited functionality that will be used for maintenance and system updates.	• Periodic maintenance is required to keep the EHR working optimally. • Scheduled downtimes will be announced in advance to allow adequate time for preparation.	• Email updates: Key dates and downtime preparation expectations • Intranet resources: Downtime planning manuals, timeline of planned updates • Decentralized meetings: Review department/unit specific downtime planning needs and considerations
7.3 Post Go-Live: New Releases and Upgrades	• Inform the organization of any major system upgrades. • Share key changes and benefits that will be realized.	• What makes this upgrade important? • Why do we need to complete the upgrade now? • Will this lay the groundwork for other steps that will follow?	• Email updates: Key features/releases and timeline • Intranet resources: References, demos, infographics, and other information to support new EHR upgrades • Roadshow presentations: Overview of what is in the future

or other groups or individuals. Whenever possible, you should share any changes that are made directly with the groups that requested them or that are most directly impacted.

 Be sure your organization has a process in place to "close the loop" and communicate with users who reported issues once their problems have been resolved. This type of functionality is often available directly through your issue reporting and/ or ticketing system. If that is the case, you should evaluate and modify default responses and messages to ensure a user-friendly experience. If you have targeted email lists or other communications channels, you may be able to push notifications to those groups who are impacted by fixes or system changes. Otherwise, if you must use broadcast email or other tools, be sure to clearly indicate what groups are impacted.

Key Objectives and Message Points

- Go-live was only the beginning of the transformation with our new EHR system.
    - Our EHR system will only reach its full potential as we continue to optimize and enhance it to work for our organization over time. This process is a long-term commitment to change that involves everyone across the enterprise and can take years to realize.
- Leaders and operational staff need to continue providing feedback and should remain engaged to ensure improvement of the EHR system over time.
    - Only with feedback and support from all areas of the enterprise will we be able to make the new EHR system work optimally, while ensuring we are meeting the collective needs of our organization.

Communications Tools

- Intranet and online
    - Intranet and other internal web pages can be helpful to share post go-live changes and updates to the EHR system.
    - Because your EHR system will likely be in a state of frequent changes – fixes, minor updates, user-requested improvements, and more – it may be difficult to keep the entire organization informed frequently without communications fatigue. Consider scheduling

a consistent time for non-emergent changes to be rolled out (e.g., every Tuesday, every other Thursday, etc.) and plan your communications timeline around that schedule.

 Encouraging staff to "seek out" or "pull" information using an intranet page, knowledgebase, or other information repository – instead of "pushing" the information to them via email – can require a culture change for some organizations. If you use a "pull" approach, be prepared to commit to long-term and frequent communications, reminding all staff that they are responsible for regularly reviewing and knowing the changes that are being shared.

   – If doing so aligns with your organization's culture and other communications activities, consider developing a theme such as "Makeover Monday" or "Transformation Tuesday" to make the schedule of regular changes easier for staff to remember.
■ Email updates
   – Consider email updates only as a secondary option for communicating system changes and updates, especially if you are making system changes frequently.
   – Email communications can be quick and easy, but overuse of them can create communications fatigue and lead to people "turning off" your message completely.
■ Web-based and classroom training
   – Consider hosting focused training programs post go-live for key end-user groups such as providers. The training sessions should focus on quick tips and guides to make documentation and other workflows more efficient. As end users get more comfortable with the new EHR, they are likely to be more receptive to new or specific features, functionalities, and tips (Example Communication 7.1).

Example Communication 7.1: Post-Live Training Program for Providers

 Title: Post-Live Training Program for Providers
Mode of Communication: Email
Target Audience: Providers
Sent from: Project Team

We are excited to announce a Post-Live training program for providers. What is included?

- As providers and staff members have started settling in with the new EHR, there have been multiple requests for additional training in both inpatient and ambulatory environments.
- The provider-focused program concentrates on improving efficiency for common activities including ordering, documentation, and using review tools, among others.
- The program is designed so that providers can leave the classroom with new tools to help them be more effective using the EHR immediately!

Who can participate?
- Sessions will be offered for providers who have been using and adjusting to the EHR for a few months.

When will sessions be held?
- The following 2-hour sessions for ambulatory providers during the week of May 23:
- Tuesday, May 23, 7–9 am and 12–2 pm
- Wednesday, May 24, 12–2 pm and 5–7 pm
- Thursday, May 25, 7–9 am and 12–2 pm
- Another round of sessions is being scheduled during the week of June 5, and more details will follow when available.

Where will sessions be held?
- The sessions listed above for May will be conducted at the IT training room.
- Future sessions are being planned to accommodate users at other campuses and locations.

Why should providers set aside two hours for post-live training?
- Sessions will equip providers with knowledge that can help them be more effective using the EHR immediately.
- Emphasis will be placed on practical tools and shortcuts to enable providers to spend more time with patients and less on documentation.

How can providers attend a session?
- Sessions require pre-registration, since space is limited.
- Providers or a designee should email EHRtraining@organization.org with the details of the session they would like to attend.
- Confirmation will be sent once a provider is registered for his or her session.

Post Go-Live: Scheduled Downtimes and Maintenance

Within the first few months following go-live, you should expect to start communicating scheduled downtimes and other maintenance needs.

Additionally, if you have an integrated EHR that is new to your organization, you will need to begin thinking about its impacts holistically. Planned downtimes can take many forms depending on the scope and duration of impact. In any case, you must be prepared for downtimes and maintenance that will require ongoing enterprise-wide communications strategies to keep staff informed in advance (Example Communication 7.2).

Example Communication 7.2: EHR Downtime Definitions

Title: EHR Downtime Definitions
Mode of Communication: Email
Target Audience: All staff
Sent from: Project Team
EHR Downtime 101

A downtime refers to a period of time when a system is unavailable due to testing, the replacement of hardware or software, or an unexpected event. During these times, the organization has contingency plans, known as downtime plans, which are put in effect by the executive team once it has become clear that the system impact may take some time to determine.
There are two basic types of downtimes:

- Planned downtimes: These are communicated in advance when EHR systems need to be routinely upgraded or maintenance needs to be performed.
- Unplanned downtimes: These can be either system failures (where a clinical system is not functioning) or a telecommunication failure (where the entire network is inaccessible).

Audiences

Prior to any planned downtime, you should ensure key groups are informed, including leaders, physicians and providers, operations, subject matter experts, and other impacted staff. If superusers or specialty provider trainers will be involved for support, ensure they are aware and have all necessary tip sheets, reference information, and resources in advance.

Key Objectives and Message Points

For system updates and maintenance, you should include the following details:

- Summary
  - What are the most important details about the planned changes or system updates?

- Who is impacted
  - What specific user groups will be affected by the downtime or other changes?
- When will this occur
  - What date and time will users be impacted?
- What this means for you
  - What are the specific impacts to the users listed above?
- What you need to do
  - Do users need to prepare or take any actions prior to the planned downtime?
- Where to get more info
  - Will tip sheets, reference guides, or other resources be made available?
- Who to contact
  - Is there a help desk or other resource to contact for questions or more information (See Example Communication 7.3)?

Communications Tools

The following tools will be helpful in communicating planned downtimes and maintenance:

- Email updates
  - Plan to send the first update at least 2 weeks prior to the planned downtime or maintenance activity. This first update should include as much detail as available.
  - Send a second email update approximately 1 to 2 days prior to the planned downtime. This update serves as a reminder for staff and will allow you to add any late-breaking details that users should know.
  - Final email updates should be sent immediately before the scheduled downtime starts and at its conclusion to confirm that normal system operations are available.
- Intranet and online
  - If your organization does not have an area established for alerts on its intranet, you should establish one and use it to post updates about scheduled downtimes and maintenance.
- Text messages
  - Text messages can be an effective way to provide real-time updates as planned downtimes are started and concluded.

Example Communication 7.3: Scheduled Downtime/Update Template

Title: Scheduled Downtime/ Update Template
Mode of Communication: Email
Target Audience: All staff
Sent from: Project Team

Scheduled Downtime/Update Template

- Consider creating a graphic header to make scheduled updates more recognizable for staff when they receive them.
- You can remove sections of information that are not needed for a specific update, but try to keep content as consistent as possible.

Summary:

- What are the most important details about the planned changes or system updates?
- Use a 1–2 sentence summary that captures the key points.

Who Is Impacted:

- What specific user groups will be affected by the downtime or other changes?
- Be sure to consider not only specific groups, but outliers who might use impacted systems.

When Will This Occur:

- What date and time will users be impacted?
- Be careful to clearly note when an impact will occur around "midnight" or "12 am" on a specific date, since the date change can cause confusion for users.

What This Means for You:

- What are the specific impacts to the users listed above?
- Be sure to include impacts for each group, if they are different.

What You Need to Do:

- Do users need to prepare or take any actions prior to the planned downtime?
- Be as specific as possible and provide tip sheets or additional guidance if detailed user actions will be required.

Where to Get More Info:

- Will tip sheets, reference guides, or other resources be made available?

- Always try to link to online resources instead of attaching them to an email, since sending files directly can result in confusion when documents change later.

Who to Contact:

- Is there a help desk or other resource to contact for questions or more information?
- Always provide an option to contact an individual or help desk group by phone and/or email in case users need to follow up.

Example Communication 7.4: Preparing for Maintenance and Planned Downtimes

Title: Preparing for Maintenance and Planned Downtimes
Mode of Communication: Email
Target Audience: All staff
Sent from: Project Team

The following checklist outlines basic tasks that all areas should ensure are verified and reviewed regularly. Doing so will help maintain a state of readiness for unplanned downtimes and ensure tools are in place for planned downtimes.

Checklist Item	Additional Details
Confirm and identify location(s) of your local/departmental downtime device(s).	This includes computers, printers and any other necessary peripheral devices.
Confirm downtime devices are labeled for easy identification.	If not, please contact the IT Solution Center to enter a ticket.
Confirm downtime devices are plugged into emergency power (red outlets) or an uninterruptible power supply (UPS).	Devices should remain plugged into emergency power or UPS <u>at all times</u>, not just during a downtime!
Confirm downtime icons are present on the desktop and that they work.	This includes printing and other web-based tools.
Confirm successful login to each downtime icon/system and that all local/departmental downtime reports print correctly.	If not, please contact the IT Solution Center to enter a ticket.
Confirm local/departmental downtime policies are updated and ready.	Policies should be current, printed, and located with the downtime device or in a designated area.
All staff members should be informed about downtime devices, policies, and workflows, as well as when any changes occur.	Managers should independently complete local education and provide updates as needed to all staff members.

Example Communication 7.5: Communications Timeline for Planned Downtimes

Title: Communications Timeline for Planned Downtimes
Mode of Communication: Email or Website Reference Materials
Target Audience: All Staff
Sent from: Project Team

Communications Timeline for Planned Downtimes

Planned Downtimes: When timing allows, all users should expect to receive a series of strategically sequenced updates prior to a planned downtime, as follows:

- Approx. 1–2 weeks before:
  - Early reminders will be given to provide an opportunity for impacted departments and areas to review, discuss, and update any downtime device or other downtime procedures as needed, or check devices, etc. to ensure operational readiness.
- Approx. 1–2 days before:
  - Final reminders will offer any "last-minute" details and confirm the planned downtime is expected to proceed according to schedule.
- Approx. 1 hour before:
  - Notifications immediately before a planned downtime will provide a brief window for users to save any current work and log out to avoid being "kicked out" when the system goes into downtime.
- Immediately after:
  - Notifications immediately after a planned downtime will confirm the final status of changes made or work done and provide users the "all clear" to log back in and begin using any impacted systems. Exceptions to normal system use will be noted.

Communications Timeline for Unplanned Downtimes

Unplanned downtimes: Because the consequences of an unplanned downtime are impossible to predict, communications will vary based on the circumstances. In general, users should expect to receive strategically sequenced updates as follows:

- Issue identification:
  - Notifications will be sent as soon as an issue has been identified and the need for user notification has been reviewed and approved by appropriate leadership.
  - Because these notifications will occur as quickly as possible when an issue has been identified, certain information, including estimated time of resolution and other specific details, might be unknown.

■ Detailed assessment:
  - Updates will be sent once an issue has been more fully analyzed to revise previous information, if needed, and provide any additional information. Based on the severity of an issue, estimated time of resolution and other details might remain uncertain.
■ Ongoing updates:
  - Timing for ongoing updates can vary from hourly to daily and will be based on the severity of an issue and the estimated timeline for resolving it.
■ Issue resolution:
  - Notifications will be provided when an issue is resolved and normal system functionality has been restored.

Post Go-Live: New Releases and Upgrades

Depending on the EHR system your organization has selected, new releases and/or significant upgrades should be expected every year or two – or more frequently. Depending on the scope and content of the release, these events can be considered minor "go-lives." They will often require some level of build, testing, training, and operational readiness activities, just as you would conduct for a full system go-live.

Key Objectives and Message Points

■ What makes this upgrade important?
  - Highlight the most important benefits that will come with the upgrade, making sure that all key audiences are addressed with at least one potential improvement.
■ Why do we need to complete the upgrade now?
  - Depending on when the upgrade is scheduled for your organization and how long it has been since go-live, there may be resistance to the additional change.
  - Be sure to focus your messaging on the importance of why this must be done now. Are there security patches that must be applied? Will new functionalities provide improvements to patient safety? Will this upgrade provide more seamless workflows for users or financial benefits for the organization?
■ Will this lay the groundwork for other steps that will follow?
  - Are there other benefits in the future that share dependencies with this upgrade? If so, lay out a high-level roadmap including the benefits that staff should expect.

Example Communication 7.6: EHR Updates

Title: EHR Updates
Mode of Communication: Email or Website Reference Materials
Target Audience: All Staff
Sent from: Project Team

There are three key types of system changes and updates:

Optimization and Enhancements:
- Changes made to help optimize or enhance how the EHR works come in many shapes and sizes. They can modify how the system looks or works, or they might require workflows in certain areas to be reviewed and revised.
- When these changes are "simple," they can sometimes be implemented with a brief "system pause" or transparently without the need for a formal planned downtime.
- More complex changes can require planned downtimes from a few minutes to several hours, in which case they are often implemented together with other updates or changes that will also require a downtime.

System Updates:
- As part of using the EHR, the Project Team will complete updates on a regular basis to patch bugs and enhance system functionality.
- You should expect updates to be delivered on a recurring basis by your EHR vendor.
- These packages can contain hundreds of changes, many of which improve system functionality in the background without visible changes to users. These changes are similar to the types of patches and updates that must be performed periodically for Microsoft Windows or any other software.

Version Upgrades:
- Upgrading from one version of the EHR to another can offer significant advances in system features and functionality.
- Consequently, version upgrades also require months of preparation, as well as additional efforts to test, train, and implement. These changes might be compared to upgrading from Microsoft Windows 8 to Windows 10.

Index